What Do You Know About Karl Marx?

What Do You Know?, Volume 2

Hichem Karoui and GEW Social Sciences and Humanities Team

Published by Global East-West LTD, 2024.

Also by Hichem Karoui

Questions
What is Happiness?
Treatise On Self-Improvement
I Have The Time

The Morning of the Mogul
The Morning of the Mogul: Arrival
James Bond in Jail
The Morning of the Mogul: Couvolution and Cooks' Conspiracy
The Muslim Brothelhood in the Bastille
Party's Gone? Patria too
The Invisible Bride
The Invisible Bride
Paradise Club Members (PCM)
Return To 'Ouja
Imbroglio

What Do You Know?
What Do You Know About Karl Marx?

Standalone
Children of Gaza
The Right To Resist
Ukraine: The Forgotten War
Shifting Sands
Guardians of the Gulf
About Albert Camus: The Man Behind the Myth
Islam And Global Politics: Understanding the Intersection of Faith and Power
Resistance As Idea And Action
Breaking the Veil: Unmasking Stigma Against Islam in the West
Angry Africa
De la Revolution au Renouveau

Watch for more at https://hichemkaroui.net/.

Also by GEW Social Sciences and
Humanities Team

What Do You Know?
What Do You Know About Karl Marx?

Table of Contents

What Do You Know?
About
Karl Marx

Hichem Karoui
And the GEW Social Sciences & Humanities Team

HICHEM KAROUI AND GEW SOCIAL SCIENCES AND HUMANITIES TEAM

Global East-West

Dedication

To the slaves of America, those before our time and those of our time,
For different reasons, of course.

Introduction

Karl Marx remains one of the most influential thinkers in history, and his ideas continue to shape our understanding of society, politics, and economics. In this book, we will delve deeper into the life, works, and impact of this remarkable writer, economist, and philosopher.

Born on May 5, 1818, in Trier, in the Kingdom of Prussia (now Germany). Marx grew up in a middle-class family with a Jewish heritage. His father, Heinrich Marx, was a lawyer, while his mother, Henriette Pressburg, came from a wealthy textile manufacturing family. Despite a comfortable upbringing and access to education, Marx's early life was marked by tragedy and upheaval. The death of his mother when he was only six years old, followed by the death of his father when he was just seventeen, had a profound impact on his worldview and intellectual development.

Marx pursued higher education at the University of Bonn and later the University of Berlin, where he studied law and philosophy. It was during his time at the University of Berlin that Marx became deeply immersed in the intellectual movements and debates of the time, particularly the ideas of Georg Wilhelm Friedrich Hegel. Hegel's philosophy, with its dialectical approach and emphasis on historical development, left an indelible mark on Marx's thinking. Marx would later incorporate and reinterpret Hegelian concepts, such as dialectical materialism, in his own works.

After completing his studies, Marx became involved in journalism and political activism, eschewing a conventional academic career. He quickly garnered a reputation for his sharp analytical skills and passionate conviction for social justice. It was during this period that

Marx met Friedrich Engels, a fellow thinker and activist, who would become his close collaborator and lifelong friend.

Together, Marx and Engels embarked on a mission to analyze and understand the conditions of the working class in the rapidly industrializing 19th century. Their research and observations formed the basis of their most influential work, The Communist Manifesto. Published in 1848, this manifesto, with its powerful call for the overthrow of the bourgeoisie and the establishment of a classless society, became an integral text for socialist and communist movements around the world.

Marx's brilliance as an economist is perhaps most evident in his magnum opus, Das Kapital. This monumental work, published in three volumes, presents a comprehensive analysis of capitalism, its origins, its contradictions, and its potential for exploitation. Marx painstakingly dissected the nature of capitalist production, arguing that the extraction of surplus value from the labor of workers lay at the heart of capitalist exploitation. Through his meticulous examination of economic systems, Marx aimed to uncover the inherent contradictions of capitalism and highlight the potential for revolutionary change.

Critics of Marx often claim that his ideas have been proven wrong or untenable due to the failures of communist regimes in the 20th century. While it is true that many of these societies did not fully align with Marx's vision, it is important to distinguish between his theoretical framework and its implementation in practice. Marx's writings sought to expose the inherent flaws and inequalities of capitalism, and his critique is still relevant today. However, the complex intersection of political, social, and economic factors in the real world cannot be reduced to a simplistic interpretation or implementation of Marx's ideas alone.

One significant aspect of Marx's theory is his emphasis on class struggle as the driving force behind historical change. Marx argued that throughout history, societies have been shaped by conflicts between social classes, primarily the owners of the means of production (the bourgeoisie) and the working class (the proletariat). This analysis provides a lens through which we can understand the power dynamics, social inequality, and the quest for social justice in various historical and contemporary contexts.

Marx's vision of a communist society, where the means of production are collectively owned, remains a topic of fervent debate. Critics often question the feasibility of such a system and point to the failures of attempts to implement it in practice. However, it is essential to recognize that Marx's ambition was to lay the groundwork for a more equitable society, and the specifics of its realization would require the active participation and agency of the working class.

Furthermore, Marx's ideas extend beyond economics and politics. His contributions to philosophy, sociology, and historiography are enduring and influential. Marx provided critical insights into the role of ideology, the alienation of labor, and the dynamics of social change. His ideas have sparked countless debates, fueled social movements, and shaped the academic landscape for generations to come.

In his philosophical writings, Marx explored the notion of alienation, arguing that under capitalism, individuals are alienated from their labor, the products they produce, and the very essence of their humanity. This concept illuminates the dehumanizing effects of a system that prioritizes profit over the well-being and self-realization of individuals. Marx highlighted how the capitalist mode of production estranges workers from the fruits of their labor, leaving them disconnected from the value they create and living in a state of constant exploitation.

Moreover, Marx's historical materialism framework emphasized the central role of material conditions and economic relations in shaping society. According to Marx, the economic base, which consists of the means of production and the social relations of production, determines the superstructure, which encompasses politics, law, ideology, and culture. This approach challenges prevailing idealist perspectives that prioritize ideas and consciousness over material conditions. Marx argued that it is changes in the economic base that ultimately drive historical transformations and societal change.

Marx's analysis of capitalism also sheds light on important issues such as the commodification of labor, the impact of technological advancement, and the inherent contradictions within the capitalist system. Marx recognized that capitalism thrives on the relentless pursuit of profit, which drives the exploitation of labor and exacerbates social inequality. The commodification of labor, where workers are treated as commodities to be bought and sold in the marketplace, turns humans into mere instruments of production, devoid of agency and dignity.

Furthermore, Marx anticipated the inherent instabilities and crises within the capitalist system. He argued that capitalism's insatiable drive for profit creates a cycle of boom and bust, leading to recurring economic crises. These crises arise from contradictions inherent in the profit-maximizing logic of capitalism, such as overproduction, underconsumption, and financial speculation. Marx's analysis provides a framework for understanding the systemic flaws and periodic disruptions that have characterized capitalist economies throughout history.

While critics may argue that Marx's ideas failed to anticipate certain aspects of modern capitalism, such as the rise of the service sector or the integration of global markets, it is important to remember that Marx's theories offer a lens through which we can continue to analyze and critique contemporary economic and social structures. Moreover, his focus on the contradictions and exploitative nature of capitalism remains valid and continues to provoke scholarly inquiry and inspire social movements seeking alternative economic and political systems.

In our contemporary era of globalization, digitization, and increasing wealth inequality, the relevance of Marx's ideas persists. The widening wealth gap, the precariousness of labor, and the concentration of power in the hands of a few have reignited interest in Marx's critique of capitalism. Moreover, questions of ecological sustainability, technological advancement, and the impact of neoliberal policies on society compel us to engage with Marx's theories in new and nuanced ways.

In the pages that follow, we will explore the profound impact of Karl Marx's ideas on the world, engaging with complex debates and exploring the ongoing relevance of his theories in contemporary society. One of Marx's key contributions is his analysis of the alienating and exploitative nature of capitalism. As we navigate a world where the pursuit of profit often comes at the expense of workers' rights, environmental sustainability, and social well-being, Marx's critique urges us to question whether the current economic system is truly serving the best interests of all.

Marx's concern for the working class and his belief in the potential for collective action and social change also resonate with current challenges and movements. Today, we witness growing discontent with income inequality, demands for fair wages and better working conditions, and the rise of grassroots movements fighting for social justice. Marx's ideas remind us that these struggles are not new, but rather part of a broader, historical struggle for emancipation.

Furthermore, as we confront pressing global issues such as climate change and the threats to our ecological systems, Marx's understanding of capitalism's relentless pursuit of profit and its disregard for environmental consequences takes on renewed significance. His analysis exposes the inherent contradictions between capitalism's need for perpetual growth and the finite resources of our planet. In this context, Marx's call for a radical transformation of the economic system is particularly pertinent.

It is worth noting that Marx's ideas have not gone unchallenged. Critics have pointed to the failures of communist regimes and the limitations of Marxist thought. However, it is crucial to separate Marx's theoretical framework from the specific historical context in which it was implemented. Marx himself did not prescribe a rigid blueprint for socialism or communism but rather provided a critical analysis of capitalism and the potential for a more equitable society. The failure of certain regimes to fully achieve Marx's vision does not invalidate the broader questions and insights he raised.

Moreover, Marx's ideas continue to inspire diverse thinkers and activists across various disciplines. From economics and sociology to philosophy and political science, his theories have prompted critical dialogue, deep analysis, and innovative approaches to understanding and transforming society. Marx's legacy extends beyond any particular political or economic system, transcending borders and ideologies. His intellectual contributions have had a lasting impact on our understanding of power, inequality, and social change.

In conclusion, Karl Marx's ideas and writings remain a significant source of inspiration and critique in our understanding of contemporary society. Despite the challenges and controversies associated with his work, his analysis of capitalism, class struggle, and the quest for social justice continues to resonate with scholars, activists, and thinkers around the world. By engaging with Marx's theories, we can deepen our understanding of the complexities of our economic, social, and political systems and contribute to the ongoing pursuit of a more equitable and just society.

Early Life and Education

Born on May 5, 1818, in the city of Trier, Germany, Karl Heinrich Marx came from a middle-class family that enjoyed a comfortable and secure lifestyle. His father, Heinrich Marx, a lawyer and a successful businessman, aspired for Karl to follow in his footsteps and pursue a career in law. Meanwhile, his mother, Henriette Pressburg, hailed from a prosperous Dutch family and provided Karl with a supportive and nurturing environment.

Growing up as the third of nine children, Marx experienced the privileges and advantages that his family's social standing afforded him. However, beneath the surface of their affluence, the Marx family faced legal and societal discrimination due to their Jewish background. This exposure to prejudice deeply impacted Marx's worldview and laid the groundwork for his later critiques of social hierarchies and inequality.

Marx's intellectual journey began at the local primary school, where his sharp mind and natural talent for learning quickly became apparent. From an early age, he displayed a voracious appetite for knowledge and was known to spend hours devouring books on various subjects. Among his favorites were history, literature, philosophy, and the socio-political issues of his time.

Inspired by his passion for learning and driven by his insatiable curiosity, Marx enrolled at the Friedrich Wilhelm Gymnasium, a prestigious secondary school in Trier, in 1830. Here, he continued to excel academically, gaining a reputation as a diligent and intellectually gifted student. Marx's deepening understanding of history, especially the struggles between classes and the dynamics of socioeconomic systems, became evident during this time.

In 1835, at the age of 17, Marx embarked on his tertiary education journey at the University of Bonn. Initially enrolled to study law, he quickly grew disillusioned with the subject and gravitated towards philosophy and literature instead. Bonn provided Marx with an intellectually stimulating environment, fostering lively discussions and debates among the students. It was during this time that Marx encountered radical ideas that would shape his thinking and set him on a path of critique and reform.

To further broaden his horizons, Marx's father arranged for him to transfer to the University of Berlin in 1836. In the German capital, Marx dedicated himself to philosophy, history, and political economy, which became the cornerstones of his intellectual development. It was during this period that Marx encountered the works of Georg Wilhelm Friedrich Hegel, a renowned philosopher whose dialectical approach to history and society left an indelible mark on Marx's thinking.

The study of Hegelian philosophy sparked in Marx a profound interest in the dynamics of historical change and the interconnectedness between ideas and social structures. Hegel's concept of dialectics, the notion that progress occurs through the clash of opposing ideas, resonated deeply with Marx. However, Marx soon departed from Hegel's idealism, which emphasized the primacy of ideas, and instead embraced materialism, grounding his theories in the material conditions and economic relationships of society.

Additionally, Marx found himself captivated by the writings of the Young Hegelians, an influential group of thinkers who questioned and critiqued the prevalent philosophical and political ideas of the time. Encounters with individuals such as Bruno Bauer and Ludwig Feuerbach challenged Marx to explore new perspectives and shaped his emerging revolutionary consciousness.

Alongside his rigorous academic pursuits, Marx became actively involved in the burgeoning political and intellectual movements in Berlin. He avidly participated in debates and engaged with various political groups, aligning himself with radical factions advocating for social and political change. Marx's enthusiasm for stirring up dissent and challenging authority often brought him into conflict with the conservative atmosphere of the university, prompting the Prussian authorities to closely monitor and suppress his activities.

In 1841, Marx completed his doctoral thesis, titled "The Difference Between the Democritean and Epicurean Philosophy of Nature." Although academic success eluded him in terms of securing a post within the university, Marx's thesis showcased his in-depth knowledge of philosophy and set the stage for his later groundbreaking works.

Faced with financial difficulties and a lack of stable employment, Marx pursued a career as a journalist in 1843. He joined the staff of the Rheinische Zeitung, a newspaper known for its critical stance against the Prussian government and its unwavering support for democratic and progressive ideas. Marx's journalistic career not only provided him a means of income but also served as an outlet for his radical beliefs and an avenue for challenging the prevailing social order.

Throughout his early life and education, it became increasingly evident that Marx possessed not only intellectual brilliance but also an unwavering commitment to his ideals. His experiences within the academic institutions, his encounters with radical thinkers, and his own personal reflections all played integral roles in the formation of his groundbreaking ideas on capitalism, class struggle, and the path towards a more equitable society. Marx's profound insights into the nature of power, exploitation, and social change would propel him into becoming one of the most influential thinkers of his time and shape the course of social and political movements for generations to come.

The Formation of Marx's Ideas

Karl Marx, one of the most influential thinkers of the 19th century, developed his ideas through a combination of intellectual influences, personal experiences, and historical conditions. The formation of Marx's ideas can be traced back to his early life and education, which played a crucial role in shaping his perspective on society and economics.

Born in 1818 in Trier, Germany, Marx grew up in a time of enormous social and political upheaval. He came from a middle-class family, with his father working as a lawyer. Marx's early education was heavily influenced by his father's insistence on classical liberal values and his mother's strong religious beliefs. These conflicting influences sparked an intellectual curiosity in Marx, driving him to question existing social structures and explore alternative ways of organizing society.

Marx pursued higher education at the University of Bonn and later at the University of Berlin, where he focused on philosophy, history, and law. These studies exposed him to various philosophical and intellectual currents of the time, including the works of Georg Wilhelm Friedrich Hegel.

Hegel's dialectical philosophy played a crucial role in shaping Marx's thinking. Hegel's dialectics emphasized the importance of historical change and the inherent contradictions within society. Marx was captivated by Hegel's concept of the dialectic, which suggests that historical progress is driven by the clash of opposing forces, leading to a synthesis that supersedes the contradictions.

However, Marx found himself dissatisfied with Hegel's idealistic approach that focused on ideas and consciousness as the driving forces of history. Marx sought to ground his theories in material reality and rejected Hegel's emphasis on the mind as the primary agent of historical change. This rejection led Marx to develop his own materialist approach, known as historical materialism.

Marx's break from Hegel became more pronounced during his involvement with the Young Hegelians, a group of left-wing intellectuals who sought to critique and reform existing social and political structures. Through his engagement with this group, Marx delved deeper into the study of political economy, including the works of Adam Smith and David Ricardo.

Smith's insights into the self-regulating nature of the market and the division of labor intrigued Marx, but he saw these as only partial explanations of the capitalist system. Marx believed that the exploitative nature of capitalism lay in the extraction of surplus value, the excess value produced by workers but appropriated by capitalists. This exploitation, according to Marx, was the foundation of class struggle and inequality within capitalism.

Building upon Ricardo's labor theory of value, Marx argued that labor was the source of all value in a commodity. He claimed that capitalists exploited workers by paying them wages that were less than the value of the goods they produced. This surplus value, accumulated by capitalists, fueled their profits and maintained the structural inequalities within society.

However, Marx's analysis of capitalism went beyond simply economic relations. He viewed societal relations as fundamentally shaped by the mode of production. In his view, the dominant economic structure determined the social, political, and cultural superstructure of a society. This materialist understanding of history became a cornerstone of Marxist thought.

Marx's exposure to the working-class struggles during his time in Paris and Brussels further shaped his ideas. He witnessed firsthand the deplorable working and living conditions of the proletariat, which strengthened his belief in the need for revolutionary change. Marx emphasized the importance of class struggle and collective action as the means to dismantle the capitalist system and establish a more equitable society.

To further develop his ideas, Marx collaborated closely with Friedrich Engels, a fellow revolutionary thinker. The two published several influential works, including "The Communist Manifesto" and "Das Kapital," which outlined their critique of capitalism and envisioned a communist society based on the principles of equality, cooperation, and the common ownership of the means of production.

Marx and Engels saw communism as a necessary response to the contradictions and crises inherent in capitalism. They believed that capitalism's relentless pursuit of profit and accumulation of wealth would inevitably lead to its downfall, as it created an unsustainable imbalance between the bourgeoisie and the proletariat. They envisioned a future society where the proletariat, through a revolution, would seize control of the means of production, eliminate private property, and establish a classless society.

Marx's ideas were not limited to economics and social theory. He also delved into political philosophy, exploring the nature of the state and its role in society. Marx argued that the state, under capitalism, served as an instrument of the ruling class, protecting their interests and upholding the existing power structures. He envisioned a socialist society where the state itself would wither away, as the need for its repressive functions would cease to exist.

In his later years, Marx devoted much of his time to the monumental work "Das Kapital." This intricate analysis of capitalist economics sought to uncover the underlying contradictions and exploitative mechanisms of the system. Although Marx was unable to complete the full series of volumes he had planned, his contributions to political economy and social theory remain an essential foundation for understanding the complexities of capitalism and its inherent contradictions.

In conclusion, the formation of Marx's ideas can be attributed to a combination of intellectual influences, personal experiences, and historical conditions. His early education, exposure to philosophy and history, engagement with political and economic theories, and direct observations of working-class struggles all played vital roles in shaping his critique of capitalism and his vision for a communist society. Marx's ideas continue to resonate and inspire researchers, activists, and scholars, prompting ongoing debates and discussions about social, economic, and political systems in the modern world.

Core Concepts of Marxism

Marxism is a complex and multifaceted theory that encompasses a wide range of concepts and ideas. At its core, Marxism seeks to analyze and critique existing social, economic, and political systems, with the ultimate goal of bringing about revolutionary change.

One of the central concepts of Marxism is the idea of class struggle. Marx argued that society is not a harmonious whole but rather is fundamentally divided into two main classes: the bourgeoisie and the proletariat. The bourgeoisie, or the capitalist class, own and control the means of production, such as factories, land, and machinery. The proletariat, on the other hand, are compelled to sell their labor to the bourgeoisie in order to survive. According to Marx, this class conflict is inherent to capitalist societies, as the bourgeoisie exploit the proletariat for their own gain. The struggle between these classes is seen as the driving force behind historical change and the potential basis for revolutionary transformation.

However, Marx also recognized that class struggle is not the only form of oppression in society. He acknowledged the interconnectedness of various forms of oppression, such as gender, race, and sexuality. Intersectionality, a term popularized by feminist scholar Kimberlé Crenshaw, has been incorporated into Marxist analysis to understand how different systems of oppression intersect and reinforce each other. Marxists argue that true liberation requires addressing all forms of oppression in an intersectional manner.

Another key concept within Marxism is historical materialism. Marx believed that the development of society and human history is shaped primarily by material conditions, such as the mode of production and the underlying economic relations. In other words, the way in which societies organize production and distribute resources determines the social structure, culture, and politics of that society. Marx argued that throughout history, different modes of production have emerged and fallen, with each mode of production giving rise to a particular set of social relations and class dynamics.

Marxism also emphasizes the notion of alienation. Marx was critical of the capitalist system for its tendency to alienate workers from the products of their labor, from their own creative potential, from each other, and from their own humanity. Within capitalism, labor becomes a commodity to be bought and sold, and workers are disconnected from the fruits of their labor, which are appropriated by the capitalist class. This alienation, Marx argued, perpetuates a sense of powerlessness and discontent among the proletariat, leading to their exploitation and ultimately fueling the desire for revolutionary change.

Central to Marxist theory is the concept of surplus value. Marx argued that under capitalism, workers are paid wages that are often only a fraction of the value they produce through their labor. The surplus, known as surplus value, is appropriated by the capitalist class as profit. Marx saw this exploitation as inherent to the capitalist system and viewed it as a source of social inequality and injustice. The extraction of surplus value from the labor of the proletariat is considered a fundamental contradiction within capitalism, leading to inequality, poverty, and the perpetuation of class divisions.

Additionally, Marxism values the notion of a planned economy and the abolition of private property. Marx proposed the establishment of a socialist society in which the means of production are owned collectively and operated in the interests of the entire community. This would involve the redistribution of wealth and power, as well as the elimination of class divisions. Marx envisioned a society in which production is planned democratically to meet the needs of all individuals, rather than being driven by profit-making motives.

Marxism also recognizes the role of ideology in maintaining the status quo and upholding the interests of the dominant class. Marx argued that the ruling ideas of any society are the ideas of the ruling class. In other words, the dominant ideas and values in society are shaped by the interests of the bourgeoisie and are used to legitimize and perpetuate their power. Marx emphasized the importance of critically analyzing and challenging these dominant ideologies in order to bring about revolutionary change.

Furthermore, Marxism highlights the role of revolution in bringing about social change. Marx believed that history is not a linear progression, but rather a series of ruptures and transformations. He argued that revolutionary action is necessary to overthrow the capitalist system and establish a socialist society. This revolutionary approach suggests that change cannot be achieved solely through legal or institutional reforms but rather requires a fundamental restructuring of power relations.

Marxism also acknowledges the importance of praxis, that is, the combination of theory and practice. Marxists believe that theory and analysis must be accompanied by action and struggle. It is not enough to simply understand the contradictions and injustices of the capitalist system; one must actively work towards its transformation. This can be seen in the various political movements that have been inspired by Marxist ideas, such as labor unions, socialist parties, and anti-imperialist movements.

However, it is important to note that Marxism has faced criticisms and adaptations over the years. Some argue that Marx's predictions of inevitable revolution have not been realized or that his analysis fails to account for the complexities of modern society. Others suggest that Marxism places too much emphasis on economic factors and neglects other forms of oppression and identity. These criticisms have led to the development of different schools within Marxism, such as feminist

Marxism, cultural Marxism, and post-Marxism, which seek to address these concerns and expand the theory's scope.

Despite its controversies, Marxism continues to be a significant force in political and intellectual discourse. Its concepts and ideas provide a framework for understanding and critiquing capitalism, inequality, and injustice. Through its focus on class struggle, historical materialism, alienation, surplus value, planned economy, ideology, intersectionality, and revolution, Marxism offers a comprehensive theory that challenges the status quo and advocates for a more egalitarian and just society.

Marxism and Revolutionary Activism

Marxism, in its essence, is not merely a theoretical framework but a call to action. The ideas and principles put forth by Karl Marx and Friedrich Engels in their works have inspired countless individuals and groups to engage in revolutionary activism. This chapter explores the deep connection between Marxism and revolutionary action, examining how Marxism provides a foundation and framework for challenging and transforming existing social and economic systems.

At the core of Marxism is the notion that all societies are divided into classes based on the ownership of the means of production. The capitalist system, according to Marx, perpetuates exploitation and alienation, with the bourgeoisie (the ruling class) dominating and oppressing the proletariat (the working class). Marx argued that the inherent contradictions within capitalism, such as the unequal distribution of wealth and the exploitation of labor, would eventually lead to its collapse.

Revolutionary activism in the Marxist tradition takes various forms, depending on the context and objectives of the movement. One of the most notable forms is the idea of the proletariat rising up against the bourgeoisie in a proletarian revolution. Marx envisioned this revolution as an inevitable outcome of the contradictions inherent in the capitalist mode of production. Proletarian revolutions aim to seize political power, abolish private ownership of the means of production, and establish a socialist or communist society. This revolution would fundamentally transform the economic, social, and political structures to create a more egalitarian and just society.

Marxism also emphasizes the importance of mass mobilization and collective action in achieving revolutionary change. Marxists argue that the working class, due to its position in the capitalist system, has the potential to bring about systemic transformation. Through strikes, protests, and other forms of direct action, workers can challenge the power dynamics of capitalism and assert their demands for better working conditions, fair wages, and overall social justice. These forms of collective action serve to disrupt the smooth functioning of capitalist society and draw attention to the inherent contradictions within it.

The concept of internationalism is another crucial aspect of revolutionary activism within Marxism. Marxists argue that capitalism is a global system, characterized by exploitation and inequality on a global scale. To challenge and dismantle this system, Marxists advocate for international solidarity among the working class. This entails recognizing that the struggle for social and economic justice is not limited to a single country but extends to all oppressed and exploited people worldwide. Internationalism, therefore, promotes unity and collaboration across borders in the pursuit of revolutionary change. Solidarity among workers across different nations strengthens their collective power, as their shared goals and aspirations transcend national boundaries.

Historically, Marxist revolutionary activism has been influential and has inspired numerous social movements and revolutions around the world. The Russian Revolution in 1917, led by Bolsheviks who drew heavily from Marxist principles, overthrew the tsarist autocracy and established the first socialist state. This event had a profound impact on subsequent revolutionary movements across the globe. The Chinese Revolution beginning in 1949, led by the Communist Party of China, resulted in the establishment of the People's Republic of China, one of the most significant socialist states in history.

However, it is important to acknowledge that not all movements and revolutions claiming to be Marxist have faithfully adhered to Marx's original ideas and principles. There have been instances where authoritarianism and oppressive regimes have emerged, distorting the ideals of Marxism. These deviations from Marxist principles have sometimes led to the consolidation of power by a ruling elite or the suppression of dissenting voices. It is important to differentiate between revolutionary movements that genuinely strive for social justice and those that appropriate Marxist rhetoric for their own ulterior motives.

Despite these challenges and distortions, the core premise of Marxism, which calls for the liberation of the working class from the shackles of capitalism, remains a powerful and enduring force. Marxism offers a critical analysis of the existing social, economic, and political systems and provides a vision for a more equitable and just society. It challenges individuals and groups to actively engage in revolutionary activism, to challenge the hegemonic power structures, and to work towards a more egalitarian future. The ongoing relevance of Marxism in the face of persistent inequalities and exploitation is a testament to its enduring appeal as a call to action for those seeking social transformation.

In conclusion, Marxism and revolutionary activism are deeply intertwined. Marxism provides a critical analysis of capitalist society and offers a vision of a classless, egalitarian future. It challenges the status quo, calling for the working class to mobilize and take revolutionary action to challenge the bourgeoisie's dominance and establish a socialist society. Through the principles of mass mobilization, internationalism, and collective action, Marxism has inspired and shaped countless revolutionary movements worldwide. While the outcomes and interpretations of these movements may vary, the call for revolutionary change remains a central tenet of Marxism, pushing society towards a more just and equitable future.

Marx's Critique of Capitalism

In his comprehensive critique of capitalism, Karl Marx delves deeply into the fundamental flaws and contradictions that define the capitalist system. For Marx, capitalism represented a mode of production and social organization that not only perpetuated exploitation but also generated inherent instability and pervasive alienation. He argued that this economic system reproduced and intensified social conflicts, inequalities, and collective suffering.

At the heart of Marx's critique lies his analysis of the exploitation of labor under capitalism. In a capitalist society, the means of production, such as factories, machinery, and land, are owned by a small group of capitalists, while the majority of the population must rely on selling their labor power for a wage. Marx's analysis of labor exploitation focuses on the extraction of surplus value: the difference between the value that workers produce through their labor and the wages they receive. This surplus value, according to Marx, is appropriated by the capitalist class, leading to the accumulation of capital and widening wealth disparities.

To understand the dynamics of labor exploitation, Marx examined the concept of labor-power commodification under capitalism. He argued that workers sell their labor-power, the ability to work, as a commodity, in exchange for a wage. However, the wage paid by capitalists does not reflect the full value that workers generate through their labor. Instead, it is deliberately set below this value to ensure profitability for the capitalist class. The surplus created by workers, which Marx labels surplus labor, is then expropriated by the capitalists as profit, enabling the further accumulation of capital.

Exploitation is not the only consequence of capitalism highlighted by Marx. He also offered a critical examination of the alienation that capitalism breeds among individuals. In capitalist production, workers are reduced to mere appendages of the production process, detached from the products of their labor. Marx identified four forms of alienation: alienation from the product, the process of production, one's own labor, and from other individuals. This sense of estrangement stems from the fact that workers have no control over the products they create, and their labor is reduced to a means of survival rather than a fulfilling and creative activity.

Moreover, Marx emphasized the inherent instability and crisis-ridden nature of capitalism. He argued that crises were not merely external shocks to an inherently stable system but rather intrinsic to the mode of capitalist production. Marx identified two main types of crises: overproduction crises and financial crises. Overproduction crises occur when the productive capacity of capitalism surpasses the effective demand for goods, leading to a surplus of unsold commodities, layoffs, and economic downturns. Financial crises, on the other hand, result from speculative investments and monetary expansion, causing asset bubbles and financial instability.

Marx saw these crises as inevitable outcomes of capitalism's insatiable drive for profit, intensified competition, and inherent contradictions. The constant pursuit of profit leads to a persistent tendency for capitalists to overinvest in production, creating imbalances that ultimately trigger economic crises. Such crises expose the vulnerabilities and contradictions of the capitalist system, revealing its inherent instability and exacerbating social inequalities.

In his critique of capitalism, Marx envisioned the emergence of a revolutionary proletarian class capable of overthrowing the capitalist order. He believed that the intensification of class conflicts and the injustices inherent in capitalism would lead to a heightened consciousness among the working class. Marx foresaw that these organized and united workers would challenge the capitalist class and seize control of the means of production. This transition from capitalism to socialism was envisioned as a fundamental restructuring of the economy, where the means of production would be collectively owned and controlled by the working class, ensuring the equitable distribution of resources and the abolition of exploitation.

Marx's incisive critique of capitalism continues to resonate and influence various fields of study, including economics, sociology, and political philosophy. While interpretations and implementations of Marx's ideas have varied, his critique provides valuable insights into the systemic flaws and injustices that persist within capitalist societies. The ongoing debates surrounding labor rights, economic inequality, and the sustainability of capitalist systems all bear the imprint of Marx's critical analysis.

Furthermore, Marx's critique of capitalism extends beyond economic analysis. It encompasses a broader understanding of social relations and power dynamics. Marx argues that under capitalism, society becomes increasingly dominated by the bourgeoisie, the capitalist class, which uses its economic power to shape political institutions and cultural norms in its favor. This concentration of power creates a society divided into two antagonistic classes, with disparate and conflicting interests.

According to Marx, the capitalist mode of production brings about a commodification of all aspects of life, as money becomes the universal measure of value. The relentless pursuit of profit undermines traditional social ties and values, transforming human relationships into mere transactions. Marx argues that capitalism reduces human worth to a monetary value, where individual worth becomes contingent on one's position within the market. In this process, social bonds erode, and individuals are alienated from each other, leading to a sense of isolation and dehumanization.

Moreover, Marx highlights the impact of capitalism on the environment. He argues that the relentless pursuit of profit and endless accumulation of capital drive the exploitation and degradation of natural resources. Capitalism's inherent need to expand and grow, coupled with its focus on short-term gains, leads to the over-extraction of resources, pollution, and the destruction of ecosystems. Marx argues that capitalism's exploitation of nature is fundamentally unsustainable, as it disregards the ecological limits of the planet.

Marx's critique of capitalism also addresses the inequalities and social stratification that arise from the capitalist mode of production. He argues that capitalism perpetuates class divisions and exacerbates social injustices. The bourgeoisie, as the ruling class, accumulates wealth and power while exploiting and oppressing the proletariat. This concentration of wealth results in a variety of social ills, including poverty, inequality, and lack of access to basic resources and opportunities.

Marx's critique of capitalism has been subject to various interpretations and criticisms over the years. Some argue that his analysis ignores the potential for innovation, technological progress, and improved living standards that capitalism can bring. Others contend that his proposed alternative, socialism, poses its own challenges and potential for abuse of power. Nevertheless, Marx's critique offers invaluable insights into the structural flaws and injustices inherent in capitalist societies, sparking ongoing debates and influencing efforts to create more equitable and sustainable systems.

The Communist Manifesto

The Communist Manifesto, a resolute and illuminating masterpiece authored by Karl Marx and Friedrich Engels, stands as an enduring testament to the power of revolutionary thought. Originally published in 1848, this seminal work of radical theory continues to resonate with individuals seeking to challenge and overthrow the prevailing system of capitalism. It serves as a rallying cry for the oppressed working class, urging them to rise against the exploitative bourgeoisie and diligently strive to establish a society free from exploitation, oppression, and the shackles of class divisions.

In the opening section of The Communist Manifesto, Marx and Engels insightfully proclaim, "The history of all hitherto existing society is the history of class struggles." Delving into the depths of human civilization's chronicles, they reveal the intricate tapestry of societies shaped by perpetual conflicts between antagonistic classes. It is within these class struggles that the foundations, structures, dynamics, and trajectory of societies are forged.

During the epochal shift of the Industrial Revolution, a transformative period marked by technological advancements and unprecedented economic growth, the bourgeoisie emerged as the ruling class, wielding a substantial concentration of wealth and commanding unrivaled control over the means of production. Through the capitalist system they championed and profited from, they relentlessly exploited the proletariat, the dispossessed working class, subjecting them to abhorrent working conditions, meager wages, and interminably long hours of labor. This exploitation was not a mere offshoot of capitalism; it was an intrinsic and inevitable consequence of its functioning.

Capitalism, as Marx and Engels astutely argue, revolutionized the world through its unwavering pursuit of profit and its relentless expansion of markets. The insatiable capitalist appetite for accumulation and expansion has effectively blurred international boundaries, establishing a global proletariat tied together by shared experiences of exploitation and suffering, intricately connected by the forces of industrialization and the inexorable spread of capitalism.

The Communist Manifesto presents communism as the antidote to the unjust and oppressive realities engendered by capitalism. Marx and Engels postulate that the system of private ownership and class divisions will ultimately sow the seeds of its own destruction. They envision a future society in which private property is abolished and the means of production are collectively owned, fostering an egalitarian system that recognizes and values each individual's contributions on an equitable scale.

Simultaneously, in their pursuit of a communist revolution, Marx and Engels outline an array of immediate measures to address the existing imbalances and establish a more just and equitable society. They advocate for the cessation of child labor, the introduction of progressive income taxation to alleviate the burdens on the working class, and the centralized control of communication and transportation systems to ensure their efficient operation for the benefit of all.

Highlighting the imperative of international solidarity among the proletariat, Marx and Engels underscore the significance of overcoming the artificial divisions imposed by ruling classes. They stress the importance of uniting the collective struggle of the working class across national borders, recognizing that only through such solidarity can the oppressive status quo be challenged and dismantled, fostering the potential for a global socialist society to emerge.

Throughout The Communist Manifesto, Marx and Engels demonstrate a keen awareness of the various criticisms and objections raised against communism. They vigorously argue that communism neither intends to erode personal freedoms nor aims to foster idleness and a lack of motivation. Instead, they contend that under capitalism, the exploitation of the majority stifles their creative potential, impeding the full development of their talents and abilities. By eliminating the inherent inequalities perpetuated by the capitalist system, communism seeks to unleash the creative energies inherent in every individual, allowing them to flourish and contribute meaningfully to society.

As the manifesto approaches its conclusion, Marx and Engels passionately call for the revolutionary overthrow of the bourgeoisie. They acknowledge the formidable challenges and significant sacrifices that lie ahead for the working class in their struggle against the exploitative forces of capitalism. However, fueled by their unwavering faith in the historical forces at play and the inherent contradictions within the capitalist system, they persistently envision a future in which the working class emerges triumphant, liberating society from the chains of exploitation and creating a world grounded in justice and equality.

The Communist Manifesto endures as an unparalleled and indomitable work of political theory, inspiring generations of revolutionaries, activists, and scholars worldwide. Its profound insights into class struggle, capitalism, and social justice continue to fuel stimulating debates and thought-provoking discussions. As humanity strives for a more equitable and just society, the teachings of The Communist Manifesto remain a continuous source of guidance and motivation, ever-relevant in the pursuit of a better future.

Das Kapital: Unraveling the Logic of Capitalism

In his seminal work, "Das Kapital," Karl Marx presents a comprehensive analysis of the capitalist system, peeling back its layers of complexity to reveal its underlying logic and intricacies. This monumental work, divided into three volumes, serves as a cornerstone of Marxist economics and a key reference for those seeking to understand and challenge capitalism.

Within "Das Kapital," Marx initiates his exploration by deconstructing the concept of commodities and the process of commodity production, aiming to demystify the seemingly innocuous objects that dominate our capitalist society. He asserts that commodities possess both a use-value and an exchange value. While use-value refers to the inherent utility or satisfaction derived from a commodity, exchange value relates to the amount of socially necessary labor time required to produce it. Marx argues that it is this labor theory of value that serves as the foundation upon which capitalism operates.

However, the analysis of the labor theory of value alone is insufficient for a comprehensive understanding of capitalist dynamics. As Marx delves further, he uncovers a fundamental contradiction within the capitalist system: the clash between the forces of production and the relations of production. The forces of production, including technology and machinery, continuously evolve, driving increased productivity and efficiency. Nonetheless, the relations of production, embodying the ownership and control of the means of production, remain in the hands of a select few capitalists. This contradiction forms the bedrock for myriad economic crises, social inequality, and the perpetuation of exploitation.

Expanding on his analysis, Marx delves deeply into the concept of surplus value, which becomes the prime source of capitalist profit. He posits that capitalists exploit the working class by paying them wages that fall short of the value they generate through their labor. The surplus value created by workers is then appropriated by capitalists, deepening the wealth divide between the bourgeoisie and the proletariat. Marx underscores that this exploitation is intrinsic to the capitalist system, creating a perpetual cycle of extraction and alienation.

In addition to exploring surplus value, Marx introduces the concept of the reserve army of labor. This reserve army consists of unemployed or underemployed workers who serve to keep wages low and ensure capitalist control over the labor force. By creating a surplus of labor, capitalists maintain a constant threat to workers, forcing them into accepting unfavorable conditions and perpetuating the cycle of exploitation.

Marx also delves into the role of capital accumulation in perpetuating the logic of capitalism. He argues that capitalists relentlessly pursue the accumulation of capital as a means of augmenting their power and influence. This pursuit spawns heightened exploitation, facilitating the concentration of wealth and economic power in the hands of a select few. Marx elucidates that this process inevitably leads to the centralization of capital, engendering the formation of monopolies that further exacerbate societal inequalities.

Throughout "Das Kapital," Marx offers a searing critique of capitalism, unearthing its inherent contradictions, exploitative nature, and devastating effects on society. He emphasizes that the logic of capitalism triggers crises, exacerbates alienation, and degrades the essence of human labor. By meticulously scrutinizing commodities, surplus value, the reserve army of labor, and capital accumulation, Marx establishes a foundation for comprehending the inner workings of capitalism and envisions the potential for revolutionary change.

Undoubtedly, "Das Kapital" ignites important debates and arouses diverse interpretations. Its analysis offers a profound lens through which to understand the complex interplay of economic, social, and political forces within capitalist societies. Whether one agrees with all of Marx's conclusions or not, "Das Kapital" remains an influential and thought-provoking masterpiece in the field of political economy, continuously inspiring further exploration and critical examination of the capitalist system.

Marx's Theory of Class Struggle

Class struggle is a central theme in the works of Karl Marx, providing a comprehensive framework for understanding the dynamics of societal change and the conflicts that arise within capitalist societies. Marx's theory of class struggle analyzes the complex interplay between different social classes and explores the ways in which these interactions shape the course of history.

Marx believed that throughout history, all societies have been divided into distinct economic classes who held conflicting interests. He identified two primary classes in capitalist societies: the bourgeoisie and the proletariat. The bourgeoisie, as the ruling class, own and control the means of production, including factories, land, and capital. Through their control over these resources, they accumulate wealth and generate profits while exploiting the labor of the proletariat.

The proletariat, on the other hand, constitutes the working class that relies on selling its labor power to the bourgeoisie in order to survive. Marx argued that the proletariat's exploitation by the bourgeoisie lays the foundation for class struggle. This exploitation occurs through a process Marx termed "surplus value," where the bourgeoisie extract more value from the labor of the proletariat than they pay in wages. This surplus value is the source of profit for the capitalists.

The inherent contradictions within capitalism create a systemic conflict between the bourgeoisie and the proletariat. As the bourgeoisie seeks to maintain its dominance and increase its profits, it intensifies the exploitation of the working class. Simultaneously, the proletarian masses, recognizing their shared experiences of exploitation and understanding their common interests, develop a class consciousness that propels them towards collective action.

Marx argued that the class struggle is not limited to economic exploitation alone but extends to political and ideological domains as well. The ruling class, through its control over key institutions such as the media, education system, and legal system, perpetuates its own ideology to maintain its power and dominance. This ideology fosters a false consciousness among the proletariat, wherein they are led to believe that their interests align with those of the bourgeoisie, thus hindering their collective action.

Marx's theory of class struggle posits that this conflict between the bourgeoisie and the proletariat is essential for driving societal change and progress. Over time, capitalism engenders an accumulation of wealth and power in the hands of a few capitalists, leading to heightened social inequality. This polarization fuels the class struggle and pushes the proletariat towards revolution.

Marx's analysis of historical materialism provides broader insights into the role of class struggle in human civilization. He argues that social change throughout history has primarily been driven by conflicts between different classes, such as the feudal lord and serf in feudal societies or the slave-owner and slave in ancient societies. Each period of history is characterized by the ruling class exploiting the labor of the subordinate class.

In the capitalist mode of production, Marx asserts that the class struggle reaches its pinnacle. The bourgeoisie not only controls the means of production but also dominates the political sphere and creates a culture that solidifies its power. The proletariat, reliant on selling their labor power and lacking ownership of the means of production, find themselves in an increasingly precarious position. The industrial revolution intensified the exploitation, leading to harsh working conditions, poverty, and alienation.

However, Marx's theory also recognizes that the ruling class will employ various strategies to counter the threat posed by the proletariat. These strategies include suppressing labor movements, fostering divisions among the working class, and developing mechanisms of social control. Nevertheless, Marx contends that the contradictions within capitalism are an intrinsic part of its functioning and cannot be fully ameliorated, ensuring that the class struggle remains a persistent force for change.

The consequence of the class struggle, according to Marx, is the ultimate overthrow of capitalism by the proletariat, leading to the establishment of a socialist society. In this new society, the means of production are collectively owned, and the exploitation of labor is abolished. Marx believed that the proletarian revolution would serve as a stepping stone towards a classless society, where social and economic inequalities are eradicated.

The theory of class struggle has been influential in shaping social movements and political ideologies, inspiring revolutions and uprisings throughout history. It has laid the foundation for the rise of labor unions, socialist and communist movements, and various forms of resistance against capitalist exploitation. While some critiques argue that Marx's theory oversimplifies the complexities of social relations, it continues to offer crucial insights into the mechanisms of power, inequality, and oppression within capitalist societies.

By understanding the class struggle, society can engage in critical analysis and work towards a more just and equitable world. Marxist concepts of solidarity, collective action, and a consciousness of class exploitation remain relevant in the fight against economic and social injustices. The ongoing struggle for a society that prioritizes the needs and well-being of all its members requires an understanding of class dynamics and the pursuit of transformative change.

Marx's Vision for a Communist Society

In exploring Karl Marx's vision for a communist society, it becomes evident that his ideas were not only a critique of the capitalist system but also a comprehensive framework for reshaping society. Marx's understanding of the capitalist mode of production went beyond its economic implications to encompass its social, political, and cultural dimensions. Through his analysis, he identified inherent contradictions within capitalism, which ultimately led to his vision for a communist society as the most just and equitable alternative.

At the heart of Marx's critique of capitalism was his observation that it commodified labor. Under capitalism, he argued, human labor became a commodity to be bought and sold, disconnecting individuals from the products of their own labor. This process of alienation resulted in a profound disconnect between workers and the fruits of their efforts, leading to feelings of powerlessness, meaninglessness, and dissatisfaction.

Marx emphasized the exploitative nature of capitalism, with its surplus value extraction from the labor of workers. Capitalists who controlled the means of production profited from the labor of the proletariat, exacerbating social inequality and class divisions. Marx believed that this inherent conflict between the bourgeoisie and the proletariat would inevitably lead to a moment of revolution, where the working class would overthrow the ruling class and take control of the means of production.

In Marx's communist society, private property would be abolished, and the means of production would be collectively owned and controlled. This collective ownership ensured that the benefits derived from production were distributed fairly among all members of society.

The guiding principle of distribution would be "from each according to their ability, to each according to their needs." By prioritizing individual needs and abilities, rather than profit margins, Marx envisioned a society where material wealth was distributed equitably, eradicating poverty and income disparities.

Furthermore, Marx believed that a communist society would eliminate the social hierarchies created by class divisions, leading to the creation of a classless society. In such a society, individuals would not be defined by their occupation or social status but rather by their shared humanity. The eradication of class distinctions would result in the dissolution of the oppressive state apparatus, which Marx believed was a tool of the ruling class to maintain their dominance. With the absence of social classes, the state would gradually wither away, as there would no longer be a need for it to manage conflicts or protect the interests of a particular group.

Marx's vision for a communist society went beyond economic and political transformations; it inherently aimed to reshape human relationships and liberate individuals from the alienation and exploitation prevalent in capitalist societies. He believed that in a communist society, individuals would have the opportunity to engage in meaningful and fulfilling work that aligns with their interests and talents. The division between mental and physical labor would be diminished, allowing workers to have a greater say in the decision-making processes of workplace management.

Furthermore, Marx argued that the inherent contradictions and crises of capitalism would be resolved within a communist society. In capitalism, the pursuit of profit often leads to economic instabilities, such as recessions and financial crises. By prioritizing social needs and collective well-being over profit, a communist society would establish a planned economy, where resources are allocated based on society's needs rather than market demands. This would enable the efficient utilization of resources and ensure the steady improvement of living standards for all members of society.

It is important to note that Marx did not provide a detailed blueprint for how a communist society would function. Instead, he recognized that the process of societal transformation would be shaped by the material conditions and historical development of each society. Marx's vision for a communist society, therefore, remains an evolving framework that encourages critical analysis and adaptation to the specific circumstances of different societies.

Although Marx's ideas have faced criticism and challenges throughout history, they continue to serve as a powerful critique of capitalism and a guiding force for socio-political movements striving for a more equitable future. Marx's vision for a communist society remains an integral part of his broader quest for a world free from class oppression, social inequalities, and alienation, providing inspiration for those seeking to build a more just and inclusive society.

Marx's Influence and Legacy

The eminent philosopher and writer, has left an indelible mark on the world with his profound ideas and writings. His intellectual contributions extend far beyond his contemporaries, and his theories have had a profound and enduring impact on various disciplines. Marx's influence on politics, economics, sociology, anthropology, history, and literature is monumental, and his ideas continue to shape the course of history and inform contemporary debates.

Marx's ideas have particularly resonated in the realm of politics, giving rise to communism and socialist movements worldwide. The Communist Manifesto, co-authored by Marx and Friedrich Engels, has provided a roadmap for revolutionary action and the establishment of a socialist society. This groundbreaking work has ignited countless revolutions and uprisings across the globe, most notably the Russian Revolution of 1917. The legacy of Marx's political thought can be seen in the establishment of socialist states such as the Soviet Union and China, which, though they deviated from Marx's original vision, sought to create societies based on his principles.

Marx's analysis of capitalism and its contradictions has significantly influenced economics and sociology. He argued that capitalism is a system marked by exploitation and alienation, where the bourgeoisie profit at the expense of the proletariat. This critique of capitalism continues to provoke discussions on income inequality, labor rights, and the role of the state in regulating economic systems. Marxist economists have developed theories that examine the dynamics of capitalist economies, such as the labor theory of value and the tendency of the rate of profit to fall. These theories continue to be debated and refined by scholars, contributing to ongoing discussions about the nature of the capitalist system.

Moreover, Marx's insights into the nature of class struggle and the dynamics of power have deeply influenced sociology. Historical materialism, a key concept in Marx's works, asserts that social relations are shaped by the material conditions of society. This framework has laid the foundation for sociological theories of social change and conflict. Marx's analysis of social class and class struggle remains an essential tool for understanding power dynamics and social inequality. Sociologists today draw on Marx's insights to analyze social transformations, class structures, and the dynamics of social movements, allowing for a more nuanced understanding of societal change.

Furthermore, Marx's ideas have permeated the field of anthropology, providing a framework for understanding cultural practices, social institutions, and societal change. Anthropologists have explored Marx's concepts of alienation and historical materialism to shed light on the ways in which economic and social systems shape human behavior, beliefs, and cultural practices. This Marxist perspective in anthropology offers critical insights into the intersections of economics, power, and culture, allowing for a comprehensive understanding of human societies across time and space.

In addition, Marx's theories have engaged literature and cultural discourse in profound ways. Writers and thinkers have employed Marx's ideas as a lens through which to explore themes of class struggle, alienation, and exploitation. Marxist literary criticism has emerged as a prominent approach, analyzing how literature reflects and reinforces societal power structures. This perspective reveals the often-hidden dynamics of social injustice and challenges readers to critically examine the dominant ideologies present in literary works. Through this lens, literature becomes more than a mere aesthetic creation; it becomes a reflection of society and an instrument for social critique and transformation.

However, while Marx's legacy is undeniable, it is not without controversies and debates. Critics argue that his ideas have been misused and manipulated throughout history, leading to authoritarian regimes, oppressive governments, and stifled individual freedoms. Some economists and political theorists challenge the practicality and viability of an entirely socialist society and present alternative models for addressing social inequality and achieving economic justice.

Despite these debates, Karl Marx's legacy as a revolutionary thinker, social critic, and influential writer remains profound. His concepts and analysis continue to shape political, economic, and social discourse around the world. Whether one agrees with his ideas or not, Marx's contributions have left an indelible mark on intellectual thought, propelling society forward in its quest for equality and justice. His work continues to inspire and challenge scholars, activists, and thinkers, cementing his place as a seminal figure in the history of ideas.

To summarize his legacy and influence is not an easy task. For Marx's ideas and writings have had a profound and lasting impact on various aspects of society, politics, and economics. His work continues to inspire and shape the thinking of scholars, activists, and policymakers around the world.

Intellectual Legacy:

a. Marx's critique of capitalism: One of Marx's most significant contributions was his scathing critique of capitalism. He argued that capitalism is exploitative and inherently unequal, as it prioritizes profit over the wellbeing of workers. Marx highlighted the alienation of labor, asserting that under capitalism, workers are separated from the products of their labor, leading to a sense of powerlessness and estrangement. Additionally, he explored the notion of commodity fetishism, arguing that in a capitalist society, goods and commodities are valued not for their use but for their exchange value. Marx's critique of capitalism laid the groundwork for subsequent analyses of the inherent contradictions and social injustices within the capitalist system.

b. Marxist analysis of class struggle: Marx proposed that history is driven by class struggle, where the dominant ruling class exploits the working class. He emphasized the importance of class consciousness and the need for the working class to organize and collectively challenge oppressive power structures. According to Marx, the bourgeoisie, as the ruling class, owns and controls the means of production, while the proletariat, the working class, only has their labor to sell in order to survive. This analysis has influenced countless activists and movements seeking to address social inequalities and achieve a fairer society.

1. Political Influence:

    a. Socialist and Communist Movements: Marx's ideas greatly influenced the emergence and development of socialist and communist movements worldwide. The Russian Revolution of 1917, led by Vladimir Lenin and the Bolshevik Party, was directly inspired by Marx's writings. It was seen as a successful attempt to put Marxist theories into practice, leading to the establishment of the Soviet Union. Marx's ideas also influenced other examples of socialist and communist experiments throughout the 20th century, including the Chinese Revolution and the Cuban Revolution. However, it is important to note that while these revolutions aligned with Marxist principles to varying degrees, they also deviated from Marx's original intentions in some aspects.

    b. Labor movements and trade unions: Marx's emphasis

on the importance of collective action and class consciousness has played a crucial role in the development of labor movements and trade unions. His theories provided the intellectual foundation for workers to unite, demand better working conditions, fair wages, and protection of their rights. The influence of Marx's ideas can be witnessed in the formation of labor unions globally, the adoption of labor laws, and the achievements of workers' rights movements. The concept of collective bargaining, which allows workers to negotiate as a group with employers, rose to prominence due to Marxist influences.

2. Economic Influence:

   a. Critique of capitalism: Marx's critique of capitalism remains highly relevant to this day. He argued that capitalism contains inherent contradictions that ultimately lead to its downfall. Marx believed that as capitalism expands, it concentrates wealth and power into the hands of a few, exacerbating inequalities and creating social unrest. He predicted that capitalism would face economic crises, the most significant being the tendency of the rate of profit to fall. While his predictions of capitalism's collapse have not come to pass as anticipated, his analysis of the structural flaws within capitalism continues to shape discussions on economic systems.

   b. Economic inequality: Marx's work on economic inequality and the concentration of wealth remains a critical aspect of his legacy. He recognized that under capitalism, wealth accumulates in the hands of a few while the majority struggle to meet their basic needs.

Marx's analysis has contributed to the understanding of income disparities and calls for wealth redistribution through progressive taxation, social welfare programs, and greater economic equity. The persistent debate on income inequality and the need for a fairer distribution of resources often draws inspiration from Marx's analysis.

3. Cultural Influence:

   a. Influence on social and cultural movements: Marx's ideas have permeated social and cultural movements, inspiring art, literature, film, and music. Themes of class struggle, social injustice, and the quest for a fairer society are common throughout cultural productions influenced by Marxism. Writers like George Orwell, through works such as "Animal Farm" and "1984," have critiqued totalitarianism and highlighted the dangers of oppressive regimes utilizing Marxist ideas. Playwright Bertolt Brecht's "Mother Courage and Her Children" explores the impact of war and capitalist exploitation on the working class, reflecting Marxist themes. The renowned Mexican artist Frida Kahlo incorporated Marxist ideas in her paintings, addressing class struggles and oppression in her works.

   b. Academic research and scholarship: Marx's ideas have become an integral component of social science research and scholarship. His theories and concepts, such as historical materialism, surplus value, alienation, and class consciousness, have provided analytical frameworks for examining power dynamics, social inequality, and societal change. Marxist analysis and theories are employed in various fields such as sociology, political science, and anthropology, contributing critical insights into the complexities of social, economic, and political systems. Scholars continue to engage with Marx's ideas, expanding and refining his theories to understand contemporary challenges and envision alternative futures.

Marx's enduring legacy and continued influence cannot be denied. While his predictions and proposed solutions may have faced criticism and challenges, his contributions to critical analysis, social justice movements, and economic discourse remain influential. Marx's brilliant intellectual abilities and deep understanding of the social and economic dynamics of his time have left an indelible mark, shaping the way we analyze, question, and seek alternatives in our modern world.

Marx in the Modern World

We owe to the truth and history to say that Marx is hated even more after his death than during his life. Some countries ban Marx and Marxist literature from their schools and Library's bookshelves, despite neither sociology nor philosophy could be fully understood without at least a glimpse on the Marxist theory, which gave birth to a significant school in sociological and philosophical theories, particularly because it is the basis of critical thinking in everything related to our contemporary society.

In the modern world, the ideas and theories of Karl Marx continue to provoke both enthusiasm and criticism, offering a profound analysis of capitalism and a vision for a communist society. Marx's theories have had a lasting impact on political and economic thought, shaping debates and movements across the globe.

One of the key aspects of Marx's work that remains relevant today is his critique of capitalism. Marx argued that capitalism is a system that is driven by the pursuit of profit, where the means of production are privately owned and exploited by the bourgeoisie, the capitalist class. He asserted that capitalism inherently produces inequalities and systematic exploitation, with the working class being oppressed by the capitalist class. Marx highlighted the alienation experienced by workers who are reduced to being mere commodities in the capitalist system, leading to class struggle.

In the modern context, economic inequality has become a significant concern of unprecedented magnitude. The concentration of wealth and power in the hands of a few elites has led to widespread discontent and social unrest. Critics argue that Marx's analysis of capitalism sheds light on the structural flaws and inherent contradictions of the system, providing insights into the causes of inequality and the need for change.

Furthermore, Marx's theories remain relevant in analyzing the challenges posed by globalization and the rise of multinational corporations. The exploitative labor practices, such as sweatshops and outsourcing, often associated with globalization, reinforce the idea of class struggle and the unequal power dynamics between workers and capitalists. Marx's emphasis on the international nature of capitalism and the need for global solidarity is particularly applicable to the contemporary world.

Moreover, Marx's concept of alienation resonates in the age of the gig economy and increasing precarity in the labor market. As workers face job insecurity, lack of control over their work, and the erosion of traditional employment relationships, feelings of alienation and detachment from the products of their labor persist. Marx's ideas offer a framework to understand these experiences and advocate for workers' rights and empowerment.

Marx's analysis of capitalism also sheds light on the ecological crisis faced by the modern world. He argued that capitalism's constant need for expansion and profit maximization is inherently at odds with sustainability and the health of the planet. The continuous extraction of resources without regard for environmental consequences is a result of the inherent logic of capital accumulation. Marx's understanding of the exploitative nature of capitalism and the need for sustainable modes of production and consumption provides a lens through which to comprehend and address the ecological challenges of our time.

Furthermore, Marx's vision for a communist society also continues to inspire and engage activists and thinkers worldwide. He envisioned a society where the means of production are collectively owned, and wealth and resources are distributed according to need. Although the implementation of communism in the twentieth century did not match Marx's ideal vision, the fundamental idea of creating a more equitable and just society endures as a goal for many.

In exploring the relevance of Marx's theories, it is important to acknowledge that his ideas have faced criticisms. Some argue that his analysis of capitalism fails to consider the transformative power of markets and innovation in raising living standards. Others point to the failures of communist regimes in the past as evidence of the impracticality or inherent flaws of Marx's ideas. Moreover, the association of Marx's theories with repressive regimes and human rights abuses has led to further skepticism and criticism.

However, what distinguishes Marx's work is its multifaceted nature and its ability to provoke critical reflection and reevaluation of societal structures. While some aspects of Marx's analysis may need adaptation or revision in light of changing contexts and historical experiences, his core insights regarding exploitation, alienation, and the dynamics of power continue to provide valuable frameworks for understanding social relations, economic systems, and historical developments.

Marx's writings have not only enriched social sciences such as sociology, political science, economics, and philosophy, but they have also influenced diverse fields, including literature, cultural studies, and even contemporary art. His concepts of labor, class struggle, and the commodification of goods have inspired countless works of literature and artistic expression that aim to represent and critique the impact of capitalism on human life and society.

The continued relevance of Marx's ideas is evident in the activism and social movements that center their demands on issues of economic justice, workers' rights, and social equality. The resurgence of interest in Marxist thought among younger generations reflects a growing dissatisfaction with the status quo and a recognition of the need for alternative frameworks to address the pressing challenges of the modern world. Marx's analysis of capitalism and his vision of a more egalitarian society continue to serve as rallying points for those seeking transformative change.

In conclusion, Marx's ideas remain relevant in the modern world, as his analysis of capitalism and proposals for a communist society continue to provoke debate and shape political and economic discussions. While his theories have faced criticisms and challenges, the enduring questions raised by Marx regarding inequality, exploitation, ecological sustainability, and the possibility of a more equitable society compel us to engage with his ideas and seek avenues for social and economic transformation. The richness and depth of Marx's analysis continue to provide valuable insights into the workings of our globalized and capitalist world, driving individuals and societies to critically examine and rethink existing systems in pursuit of a more just and inclusive future.

Criticisms and Misinterpretations of Marx

Karl Marx's ideas have faced their fair share of criticisms and misinterpretations. These range from ideological disagreements to scholarly debates regarding the practical implications of his theories. While not all criticisms are founded on a thorough understanding of Marx's works, they have contributed to shaping the perception of his ideas and their application.

One common criticism of Marx's theories is the claim that his ideas lead to authoritarian regimes and totalitarian governments. Critics argue that the implementation of Marxist ideas in countries such as the Soviet Union, China, and North Korea resulted in oppressive regimes. However, it is essential to note that Marx himself did not prescribe or envision these forms of governance. He emphasized the importance of the working class leading the revolution and advocated for a stateless, classless society. Therefore, attributing the actions of such regimes solely to Marx's ideas can be seen as a misinterpretation.

It is vital to distinguish between Marx's original theories and the interpretations and adaptations they have undergone in various political contexts. The adoption of Marxism by totalitarian regimes often involved significant deviations from Marx's intended objectives, as these regimes consolidated power and suppressed dissent. Marx envisioned communism as a system that allowed for the mutual liberation of individuals, not one that imposed a new form of oppression. Therefore, to criticize Marx based on the actions of these authoritarian regimes is to misrepresent his core ideas and their potential outcomes.

Another criticism often directed towards Marx is the notion that his theories undermine the importance of individual liberty and personal freedom. Some argue that Marx's focus on the collective and the subordination of individual interests neglects the value and autonomy of the individual. However, Marx's concern with class struggle and the oppressive nature of capitalism was aimed at addressing the systemic inequalities that restrict individual freedoms. He saw communism as a means to liberate individuals from the exploitative conditions of capitalism, allowing them to pursue their interests more fully.

Marx recognized that true individual freedom is best achieved within a just and equitable society. He argued that capitalism, with its inherent class divisions and exploitation of labor, curtailed the freedom of the working class. By advocating for a system that seeks to eliminate such exploitation, Marx aimed to create conditions that would maximize the potential for individual self-realization and autonomy. Thus, the critique that Marx's ideas undermine individual freedom fails to acknowledge the context in which he developed his theories and the objective of his critique of capitalism.

Dissenters also question the feasibility of Marx's theory of surplus value and the labor theory of value. Critics argue that these concepts overlook the complexities of market dynamics and the role of supply and demand in determining value. They assert that the subjective theory of value, which suggests that the worth of a good or service is determined by consumer preferences and utility, provides a more accurate understanding of value.

While it is true that Marx's theories on value focus primarily on the labor invested in production, it is important to recognize that he did not disregard other factors that influence price formation. Marx's labor theory of value intended to uncover the exploitative nature of the capitalist system, where the surplus value created by workers is appropriated by capitalists. It aimed to shed light on the underlying power relations within capitalist societies and critique the unequal distribution of wealth.

Furthermore, critics often contend that Marx's theories oversimplify human nature and fail to account for the diversity of human motivations and aspirations. They argue that humans are driven by more than just economic factors, such as the pursuit of happiness, personal fulfillment, and creativity. While it is true that Marx's theories primarily focus on the economic aspects of human behavior, they aim to uncover the underlying socioeconomic structures that shape human conditions and possibilities. By critiquing capitalism's impact on the working class, Marx sought to create a society that would enable individuals to fully realize their potential.

Marx acknowledged the complexity of human nature but argued that economic relations play a significant role in shaping societal structures and individual behavior. His examination of class struggle and the dynamics of capitalism aimed to highlight the systemic barriers and limitations that hinder the realization of human potential. In addressing these structural issues, Marx sought to create a society that would allow for the fullest expression of human creativity, aspirations, and personal fulfillment.

Lastly, Marx's writings have been criticized for their complexity and ambiguity, leading to various interpretations and misinterpretations. Some argue that his works are too dense and require extensive study to fully grasp their meaning. This complexity has resulted in both insightful analyses and misinterpretations of his ideas. However, it is essential to approach Marx's writings with a critical and comprehensive understanding, considering the broader socio-political context in which he developed his theories.

Understanding Marx's works requires a multidisciplinary approach that encompasses economics, sociology, history, and political philosophy. Delving into his writings allows for a deeper understanding of the structural critique he made of capitalism and the implications for societal transformation. It is also crucial to acknowledge that Marx's ideas evolved over time, and his later works challenging traditional Marxist interpretations have influenced subsequent schools of thought.

Marx's concept of alienation, for example, is often underappreciated but nonetheless crucial to understanding his critique of capitalism. In exploring the concept, Marx argued that under capitalism, workers are disconnected from the products they create, the process of production, their fellow workers, and even themselves. This alienation arises from the capitalist mode of production, where workers are reduced to mere appendages of the machinery, carrying out repetitive tasks without a sense of fulfillment or meaningful engagement.

Furthermore, Marx's analysis of dialectics, historical materialism, and class struggle provides a framework for understanding the historical trajectory of societies and the dynamics of social change. By recognizing the dialectical relationship between opposing forces and material conditions, Marx highlighted the inherent contradictions within capitalist society that lead to its development and eventual transformation.

While critiquing Marx's ideas, it is crucial to recognize his contributions to social and political thought. Marx challenged prevailing notions of political economy, shed light on the exploitative nature of capitalism, and offered a conceptual framework for understanding power relations and class struggle. His theories continue to inspire critical thinking, academic research, and movements advocating for social justice and equitable societies.

In conclusion, while Karl Marx's theories have faced criticism and misinterpretation, it is crucial to engage with his ideas in a scholarly and comprehensive manner. Such analysis allows us to appreciate the nuances of his critique of capitalism, his vision for a more equitable society, and the enduring relevance of his analysis of socioeconomic structures. Only through rigorous study and critical analysis can we move beyond simplistic misinterpretations and develop a nuanced understanding of Marx's contributions to the realms of economics, sociology, and political philosophy.

Critiques and Controversies Takeaways

1. Economic Critiques: Marx's economic theories have been the subject of numerous critiques regarding their validity and applicability. One significant area of criticism revolves around the belief that Marx's analysis of capitalism is overly simplistic and fails to consider the complexities and nuances of the market system. Critics argue that his prediction of the inevitable collapse of capitalism has been proven wrong, as capitalism has shown remarkable resilience and adaptability.

Critics contend that Marx's understanding of the capitalist system disregards the role of entrepreneurship, innovation, and technological advancements in driving economic growth. They argue that capitalism, through the profit motive and competition, incentivizes efficiency and productivity, leading to increased standards of living for many people. They also emphasize the role of market dynamics in allocating resources efficiently and distributing goods and services based on consumer demand.

Additionally, some economists criticize Marx's labor theory of value, which states that the value of a commodity is determined solely by the amount of socially necessary labor time required to produce it. Critics claim that value is determined by more than just labor, but also by scarcity, utility, and subjective preferences. They highlight that the market price of a good or service is determined by supply and demand dynamics, rather than solely the amount of labor invested.

Furthermore, critics argue that Marx's focus on the exploitation of labor fails to recognize the potential benefits of wage labor for workers. They contend that wage labor offers opportunities for skills development, access to capital, and upward mobility, challenging the notion that all forms of labor under capitalism are inherently oppressive.

2. Political Critiques: Marx's political theories, particularly the concept of the dictatorship of the proletariat, have faced significant criticism as well. Critics argue that this concept inevitably leads to authoritarian regimes, as it concentrates power in the hands of a few individuals who claim to represent the proletariat. They raise concerns about the potential for abuse of power and the suppression of individual liberties in such a system.

Moreover, critics claim that Marx's revolutionary approach ignores the potential for incremental change and reform within the capitalist system. They argue that gradual improvements and social reforms, combined with a democratic framework, can alleviate social inequalities without the need for a violent overthrow of the existing system. They emphasize the importance of democratic institutions, checks and balances, and respect for individual rights in achieving a more equitable society.

Additionally, critics highlight the failure of Marxist-Leninist regimes in the 20th century to uphold democratic ideals and protect human rights. They argue that the implementation of socialism under these regimes led to totalitarianism, repression, and economic inefficiencies, further undermining the viability of Marxist political principles.

3. Social Critiques: One prevalent critique of Marxism revolves around the allegation that it fails to sufficiently address issues of identity, such as race, gender, and sexuality. Critics argue that Marx's focus on class struggles tends to ignore the ways in which other forms of oppression intersect with economic exploitation. They assert that a more comprehensive analysis must take into account the ways in which multiple systems of power operate simultaneously, acknowledging the importance of social identities and intersectionality.

Critics also highlight the limitations of Marx's analysis when it comes to understanding the role of culture and ideology. They argue that Marxist theory places too much emphasis on material factors, such as economic relations, while undervaluing the influence of ideas, cultural values, and ideologies in shaping societal dynamics. They contend that a more holistic approach is necessary, one that integrates cultural, political, and economic factors to comprehensively analyze social phenomena.

Furthermore, some critique Marx's concept of alienation for its lack of consideration for the individual experience and subjective well-being. Critics argue that Marx's emphasis on collective liberation neglects the importance of individual agency, creativity, and fulfillment. They propose the integration of psychological and sociological perspectives to understand the complexities of human experience and the pursuit of happiness within a socioeconomic context.

4. Historical Critiques: Marx's historical materialism, which argues that the development of society is driven by changes in the mode of production, has faced scrutiny from critics. They argue that this approach overlooks the influence of ideas, culture, and other non-material factors in shaping historical developments. They stress the importance of understanding various factors, including ideology, cultural values, and technological advancements, in analyzing historical processes and societal changes.

Moreover, critics contend that Marx's deterministic view of history, which posits an inevitable progression towards communism, fails to account for the complexities of human agency and the unpredictable nature of historical events. They argue that historical outcomes are contingent upon a multitude of factors, including human choices, collective actions, and external contingencies. This perspective suggests that historical development is not predetermined but shaped by numerous intersecting forces, challenging Marx's teleological understanding of history.

In addition, some critics point out that Marx's analysis primarily focuses on Western capitalist societies and neglects non-Western experiences and divergent historical paths. They argue that applying Marx's theories universally overlooks the unique historical, cultural, and social contexts that shape different societies and their economic systems.

5. Contemporary Relevance and Debates: The relevance of Marx's ideas in the contemporary world remains a topic of debate. Critics argue that the collapse of communism in the Soviet Union and other Eastern Bloc countries discredits Marx's theories and validates the superiority of capitalism. They contend that the end of the Cold War signifies the triumph of liberal democracy and market economies, emphasizing the role of individual freedoms, market efficiency, and the potential for technological progress in promoting social welfare.

However, proponents of Marx's ideas assert that his analysis of capitalism remains relevant in understanding and critiquing the inequalities and contradictions of the current global economic system. They point to rising income disparities, exploitative labor practices, and environmental degradation as evidence that Marx's critique of capitalism still holds true today. These proponents advocate for a more equitable and sustainable economic system that addresses societal needs, protects the environment, and prioritizes social well-being over the pursuit of profit.

Despite the critiques and controversies surrounding Marx's theories, his contributions to social and economic thought continue to shape intellectual discourse and inspire debates about alternatives to the current socio-political order. The ongoing engagement with Marx's ideas reflects a commitment to critical analysis and an exploration of new possibilities for creating fairer, more just, and inclusive societies.

Marx's Relevance in the 21st Century

As we enter the 21st century, the ideas of Karl Marx continue to provoke lively discussions and debates. Marx's critique of capitalism and his vision for a communist society may seem like relics of the past, but upon closer examination, his theories remain highly relevant in today's world. In this chapter, we will explore the enduring relevance of Marx's ideas and how they can help us understand and navigate the challenges of the 21st century.

The Persistence of Capitalist Inequality:

One of the key aspects of Marx's analysis of capitalism was his focus on the inherent inequality it produces. Despite advancements in technology and globalization, we still witness stark economic disparities across the globe. The wealth gap between the rich and the poor continues to widen, with a small minority controlling a disproportionate amount of resources and power. Marx's insights remind us that capitalism tends to perpetuate and exacerbate this inequality, prompting us to question and challenge the prevailing economic system.

Marx argued that capitalism inherently creates class divisions between the bourgeoisie (the capitalists who own the means of production) and the proletariat (the working class). He believed that capitalism thrives on the exploitation of labor, as the bourgeoisie pay workers wages that are usually not proportional to the value they generate through their labor. As a result, the rich continue to accumulate wealth, while the working class struggles to make ends meet. This analysis remains relevant in the 21st century, where income inequality persists and the gap between the rich and the poor shows no signs of narrowing.

The contemporary context further reveals new dimensions of capitalist inequality. The rise of gig economy platforms, such as Uber and Airbnb, has deepened precarity for workers by shifting the burden of risk onto individuals without providing the benefits and protection associated with traditional employment. This new form of exploitation points to the continued relevance of Marx's analysis of labor exploitation and the need for comprehensive protections for workers in the face of evolving capitalist structures.

The financialization of the economy, with its emphasis on speculative practices and the accumulation of wealth through the manipulation of financial instruments, has also intensified inequalities. Marx's concept of fictitious capital, which refers to the creation of wealth through derivative securities disconnected from tangible assets, allows us to understand how the financial sector extracts value from the real economy. The 2008 global financial crisis exposed the ramifications of this phenomenon, with the wealthy few being bailed out while ordinary people suffered the consequences. Marx's analysis provides us with a critical framework to examine these mechanisms of the financial system and advocate for regulations that prevent widespread economic crises and reduce inequality.

Globalization and Exploitation:

In the era of globalization, Marx's ideas about the exploitation of labor remain highly relevant. Transnational corporations often take advantage of cheap labor in developing countries, paying workers meager wages and subjecting them to hazardous conditions. Marx's analysis sheds light on the dynamics of exploitation and the concentration of wealth in the hands of a few, forcing us to confront these injustices and strive for fair and equitable labor practices.

Globalization has led to the globalization of exploitation, where companies seek to maximize profits by locating production in countries with lower labor and environmental standards. This race to the bottom drives down wages and working conditions, benefiting multinational corporations at the expense of workers in both developed and developing countries. Marx's analysis of the exploitation of labor allows us to understand these global dynamics and highlights the need for international solidarity to fight against this exploitation.

Moreover, the digital revolution and the emergence of the platform economy have unveiled new forms of exploitation. Companies like Amazon and gig economy platforms rely on algorithmic management and surveillance to control and exploit workers. This "algorithmic exploitation" goes beyond the traditional employer-employee relationship, as algorithms dictate work schedules, wages, and conditions. Marx's theories help us comprehend the mechanisms behind this digital exploitation and inspire us to advocate for labor protections and algorithmic transparency to safeguard workers' rights.

Environmental Crisis and Alienation:

Marx also anticipated the environmental repercussions of capitalism, particularly its exploitative and extractive nature. The 21st century has brought to the forefront the pressing issue of climate change and the destruction of natural habitats. Through Marx's lens, we can understand how capitalism sees nature solely as a resource to be exploited for profit, leading to the alienation of humans from the environment. Marx's ecological critique urges us to consider alternative modes of production that prioritize sustainability and ecological harmony.

Today, the ecological crisis has reached unprecedented levels with rapid deforestation, species extinction, and climate change caused by unrestrained capitalist production. Marx's analysis can help us recognize that the capitalist system's relentless pursuit of profit puts short-term gains above long-term sustainability. By adopting Marx's ecological critique, we can challenge the prevailing growth-oriented economic model and strive for sustainable practices that promote the well-being of both humanity and the natural world.

Marx's concepts of metabolic rift and alienation shed light on the detrimental effects of capitalist production on the environment and human well-being. The alienation of workers from the products of their labor, from other workers, and from the natural world under capitalism contributes to an exploitative and disconnected relationship with nature. Marx's ideas encourage us to reevaluate our relationship with the environment and envision a society that values ecological balance and stewardship.

Technological Advancements and Automation:

Advancements in technology, such as artificial intelligence and automation, have raised concerns about job displacement and the future of work. Marx's theory of the labor theory of value helps us understand the impact of automation on the working class and the potential for increased inequality. By grappling with Marx's concepts, we can critically analyze the social and economic implications of technological progress and strive for a future that prioritizes human well-being over profit.

The rise of automation in the 21st century has led to fears of widespread job loss and increased inequality. Marx's labor theory of value highlights how capitalism, driven by the pursuit of profit, prioritizes the efficient use of technology to reduce labor costs, often at the expense of workers. This analysis allows us to question the current trajectory of technological advancements and advocate for a society where technological progress benefits all members of society, rather than concentrating wealth and power in the hands of a few.

Alongside the concerns of job displacement, Marx's theory of alienation provides insights into the potential consequences of technological advancements on workers' sense of fulfillment and purpose. As automation increasingly replaces human labor, there is a risk of exacerbating the alienation of workers from their creative potential and intrinsic satisfaction derived from labor. Marx's ideas push us to critically evaluate the impact of technological advancements on the quality of work and advocate for a future where automation is aligned with the liberation of human creativity rather than its suppression.

Social Movements and Class Struggle:

Marx's theory of class struggle provides a framework for understanding social movements and their demands for justice and equality. In the 21st century, we have witnessed various movements that challenge the status quo, such as movements for racial justice, gender equality, and workers' rights. By drawing on Marx's analysis, we can recognize the underlying power dynamics and systemic injustices that fuel these movements and work towards creating a more inclusive and equitable society.

Marx's concept of class struggle remains relevant in the 21st century, as various social movements bring attention to issues of systemic oppression and inequality. Movements like Black Lives Matter, feminist movements, and labor movements all highlight the need for structural change and challenge the power structures that perpetuate inequality.

Marx's analysis helps us understand the interconnectedness of these social movements and their shared goal of dismantling the capitalist system and achieving a more equitable society. By recognizing the common struggles and oppressions faced by different marginalized groups, we can work towards solidarity and collective action to challenge the structural inequalities ingrained in capitalist societies.

For instance, Marx's analysis of the commodification of labor and exploitation can inform our understanding of the struggles faced by workers, particularly those in precarious and low-wage jobs. Labor movements, inspired by Marx's ideas, advocate for fair wages, better working conditions, and workers' rights. By framing these struggles as a form of class struggle, we can unite different sectors of the working class and push for systemic change.

Similarly, Marx's analysis of the role of ideology and false consciousness helps us understand the ways in which dominant narratives and ideologies perpetuate inequalities and maintain the status quo. Movements for racial justice, for example, challenge the racialized inequalities ingrained in capitalist societies and question the dominant narratives that perpetuate systemic racism. By drawing on Marx's insights, we can critically examine the ways in which capitalist systems perpetuate and reinforce racism and work towards dismantling these structures.

In conclusion, Karl Marx's ideas remain relevant in the 21st century as we grapple with persistent inequalities, global exploitation, environmental crisis, technological advancements, and social movements for justice and equality. Marx's analysis provides us with critical frameworks to understand and critique the capitalist system and envision alternative modes of production and social organization. By engaging with Marx's theories, we can challenge the prevailing economic and social order and work towards a more equitable and sustainable future.

# Conclusion: Engaging with Marx's Ideas

Having meticulously explored the life, ideas, and transcendent legacy of Karl Marx, it becomes impossible not to be captivated by the profound impact he has had on the social sciences, philosophy, politics, and even literature. Marx's analysis of capitalism, his theories of class struggle, and his vision of a communist society have left an indelible mark on intellectual thought, social movements, and political ideologies throughout the history of humankind.

To truly immerse ourselves in the profoundly transformative nature of Marx's ideas, it is imperative to delve even deeper into the intricacies of his writings and contextualize them within the historical and philosophical traditions that molded his thinking. Born in 1818 in Trier, Germany, Marx came of age during a tumultuous period of immense upheaval as Europe witnessed the gradual and often turbulent transition from feudalism to capitalism, accompanied by unprecedented levels of industrialization and urbanization. These profound socio-economic transformations served as the fertile ground on which Marx's intellectual development blossomed, propelling him to critique the capitalist system and expose its inherent contradictions.

Marx's monumental work, "Capital," unveils the enigmatic mechanisms of capitalism, laying bare its exploitative nature with unparalleled precision. He argues that capitalism is driven by the ceaseless pursuit of profit, which in turn leads to the commodification of labor and the alienation of workers from the fruits of their labor. Yet, Marx's analysis reaches far beyond mere observation, as he provides a comprehensive theoretical framework to understand the intricate dynamics of class struggle, surplus value extraction, and the inherent instability plaguing the capitalist mode of production.

Delving even deeper into Marx's ideas, we must acquire a nuanced understanding of his conception of class. For Marx, class struggle was the mighty locomotive propelling historical change. While he primarily identified the bourgeoisie, the owners of capital, and the proletariat, the exploited working class, as the primary antagonistic classes within capitalist societies, he acknowledged that the structure of classes could be far more complex and fluid. Additional layers of social strata, such as the petite bourgeoisie, intellectuals, and the lumpenproletariat, played significant roles in shaping the social fabric and the dynamics of mobilization and resistance.

A crucial aspect of deeply engaging with Marx's ideas lies in recognizing the diverse interpretations and adaptations that have emerged across various contexts and historical moments. From the Russian Revolution to the plethora of socialist and communist movements that have emerged worldwide, Marx's ideas have been modified, adjusted, and sometimes even misappropriated to fit specific social, political, and historical circumstances. This astonishing variety of interpretations should encourage us to approach Marx's ideas with openness and intellectual humility, recognizing both the measure of their profundity and the potential limitations and pitfalls stemming from any single interpretation.

Furthermore, delving into a profound engagement with Marx's ideas compels us to examine their continued relevance in the complex landscape of the 21st century. Since Marx's era, capitalism has continually evolved, adopting new forms and adapting to the challenges posed by globalization, technological advancements, and the ever-deepening interconnectedness of our world. From the rise of neoliberalism to the emergence of financialization and emerging digital economies, contemporary capitalism presents a tapestry of complex dynamics that demand a critical reevaluation of Marx's theories. While insights on exploitation, inequality, and alienation remain ever-present in our socio-economic fabric, in-depth explorations are required to update and expand Marx's conceptual framework to address the myriad complexities of today's economic, political, and cultural realities.

Thus, in the years since Karl Marx's death, his ideas and theories have continued to shape and influence numerous aspects of the modern world. Despite initial opposition and misconceptions, Marx's works have become essential in understanding society, economics, politics, philosophy, and culture.

One of the significant areas where Marx's ideas remain relevant is in the realm of economics. Marx's critique of capitalism still resonates with many scholars and activists who argue that the system perpetuates inequality and exploitation. His concept of class struggle, which posits that society is divided into two main classes, the bourgeoisie and the proletariat, continues to be studied and applied in analyzing contemporary economic disparities and social tensions.

Marx's labor theory of value, which suggests that the value of a commodity is determined by the amount of socially necessary labor required to produce it, has also left a lasting impact on economic thought. Although this theory has been subject to debates and revisions, it has contributed to our understanding of the relationship between labor, value, and profit within capitalist systems. Marx's concept of surplus value, which refers to the excess value created by workers that is appropriated by capitalists, provides a critical lens to analyze exploitation in the capitalist mode of production.

Moreover, Marx's writings on capitalism's inherent contradictions and crises have gained renewed significance in recent years. With the global financial crisis of 2008 and subsequent economic shocks, many have questioned the stability and fairness of capitalism. Economists and scholars have revisited Marx's analysis of the tendency of the rate of profit to decline and his predictions of cyclical economic crises. These discussions highlight the ongoing relevance of Marx's economic theories in understanding contemporary capitalist economies.

Marx's ideas have also had a profound impact on the field of sociology. His emphasis on the social structures and relations that shape human behavior provides a foundation for understanding social inequalities, power dynamics, and social change. Marx's concept of alienation, which refers to the separation of individuals from the products of their labor and from their true human essence, is still highly relevant in modern society. It helps explain the feelings of disconnection and dissatisfaction often experienced by workers in highly specialized and dehumanizing occupations.

Furthermore, Marx's theories of social class and power structures have influenced various sociological perspectives, including conflict theory and critical theory. These perspectives highlight the unequal distribution of power and resources in society and seek to challenge and transform social systems that perpetuate oppression and inequality. Marx's writings continue to inspire sociological research and activism aimed at addressing social injustices and seeking social change.

Marx's critique of imperialism and colonialism has also remained relevant in understanding global power dynamics. His analysis of how capitalism exploits resources and labor in underdeveloped regions still informs discussions on neocolonialism and global inequality. Marxist scholars argue that capitalism's drive for accumulation and expansion drives it to extract resources and exploit labor from countries in the Global South, perpetuating global power imbalances. Marx's writings continue to inspire anti-imperialist and anti-colonial movements around the world.

Another crucial area where Marx's influence is felt is in politics and social movements. Marxist ideas have played a significant role in the formation and development of socialist and communist movements. The Bolshevik Revolution in Russia, led by Vladimir Lenin, was deeply influenced by Marx's works, as were subsequent communist movements globally.

Marx's theories also continue to inspire a range of left-wing social and political movements, including labor movements, anti-globalization campaigns, and social justice movements. The principles of equality, worker empowerment, and social transformation advocated by Marx provide a basis for critique and mobilization against capitalist exploitation and inequality. Although diverse interpretations and adaptations of Marxism exist, the central themes of Marx's ideas continue to guide those working for societal change and progressive transformation.

However, Marx's theories have also been subject to various criticisms and debates. Some argue that his predictions about the feasibility and prospects of socialism and communism have not materialized as he envisioned. Critics question the practicality and sustainability of Marxist political and economic models, pointing to historical instances of authoritarianism and economic inefficiency associated with some Marxist-inspired regimes. Despite these critiques, Marx's ideas continue to inspire activism, social movements, and progressive political thought worldwide.

In recent years, there has been a resurgence of interest in Marx's writings, particularly among younger generations. The global financial crisis of 2008 and subsequent economic and social struggles have led many to question the foundations of capitalism and turn to Marx for insight and alternatives.

Moreover, Marx's analysis of the contradictions and crises inherent in capitalism has been seen by some as prescient in light of the contemporary challenges faced by our globalized, neoliberal world. The growing wealth gap, environmental degradation, and the precariousness of labor have renewed debates around Marx's ideas as potential solutions to these problems.

Academic disciplines such as philosophy, anthropology, and cultural studies also continue to engage with Marx's theories, examining their relevance to understanding social and cultural phenomena. Marx's ideas have made significant contributions to the understanding of power dynamics, ideology, and cultural production, influencing critical theories that analyze social structures, cultural practices, and societal norms.

Furthermore, Marx's writings have inspired feminist theorists to examine the gendered dimensions of capitalist exploitation and to explore how patriarchy intersects with class struggle. Intersectional approaches that incorporate Marx's theories allow for a more nuanced understanding of the ways in which capitalism perpetuates multiple forms of oppression.

Marx's ideas have also had an impact on environmental studies, as his analysis of capitalism's insatiable drive for profits and disregard for ecological limits parallels concerns about climate change and environmental degradation. Scholars have incorporated Marx's insights into critical ecological economics and political ecology, emphasizing the need to challenge capitalist modes of production that prioritize growth over sustainability.

In summary, Marx's ideas and theories have remained relevant and influential in the modern world, permeating various academic disciplines and influencing social movements. His critique of capitalism, analysis of social structures, and emphasis on social change continue to provide a lens through which we can understand and navigate the complexities of contemporary society. Marx's works inspire ongoing debates, activism, and scholarship, making him a crucial figure in shaping our understanding of the modern world.

Engaging with Marx's ideas should not be a passive engagement; it necessitates active participation in shaping the future and the course of history. Marx perceived individuals as agents of transformative change, emphasizing the revolutionary consciousness and collective agency as vehicles for challenging the status quo and constructing a more equitable society. As we dedicate ourselves to engaging with Marx's ideas, our task remains not only to analyze his theories and elucidate their inner workings but also to wholeheartedly participate in ongoing debates on social and economic justice, identifying new avenues for change and ensuring our actions resonate with the principles of inclusivity, egalitarianism, and respect for human rights.

Finally, delving into Marx's ideas in a profound manner is an intellectual journey that demands deep immersion in his writings, meticulous understanding of the historical context that shaped his theories, critical evaluation of their applicability across diverse contexts, and active participation in the ongoing quest for a more just and equitable future. By engaging with Marx's ideas in such a profound manner, we perpetuate the legacy of a remarkable thinker and enrich the ongoing struggle for social and economic justice in our ever-changing and unpredictable world.

Post-Scriptum

The emergence of industrial capitalism in the 19th century brought about significant changes in society, particularly for the working class. In order to fully understand the conditions they faced, it is essential to delve deeper into the works of Karl Marx and Friedrich Engels, two influential figures whose writings shed light on the injustices perpetuated by this new economic system. This chapter will explore their theories and analyses, uncovering the harsh realities experienced by the working class and the inherent contradictions of capitalism.

Marx, in his seminal work "Capital: Volume I," meticulously examined the capitalist mode of production. He argued that capitalism exploits the labor power of the working class, resulting in a fundamental conflict between the bourgeoisie, who own the means of production, and the proletariat, who must sell their labor in order to survive. According to Marx, the relentless pursuit of profit drives capitalists to exploit workers by paying them low wages and subjecting them to harsh working conditions.

Engels, in "The Condition of the Working Class in England," provided a vivid and haunting account of the deplorable living and working conditions endured by the proletariat. He exposed the appalling housing conditions, overcrowded slums, and unsanitary environments that were the direct consequences of unrestrained capitalist practices. Engels revealed the social and physical degradation faced by the working class, highlighting the stark contrast between the opulence of the bourgeoisie and the misery and deprivation experienced by the masses.

Central to Marxist thought is the concept of alienation. Marx argued that in capitalist societies, workers are alienated from the product of their labor, as they have no control or ownership over what they produce. Instead, the products become commodities, controlled and profited upon by the bourgeoisie. This alienation extends to the process of labor itself, as workers are reduced to mere cogs in the industrial machinery, devoid of creativity and fulfillment. Furthermore, workers are alienated from their fellow human beings, as the capitalist system fosters competition and individualism rather than cooperation and solidarity.

Marx and Engels also emphasized the cyclical nature of capitalism, marked by economic crises and the overproduction of goods. They argued that these crises are inherent in the capitalist system, resulting from its insatiable drive for profit and the contradictions between labor and capital. During such crises, the working class suffers the most, facing unemployment, wage cuts, and increased poverty, while the capitalists strive to protect their wealth and maintain their power.

Critics may argue that the Marxist critique of capitalism oversimplifies the complexities of the economic system and disregards the potential for individual success within it. However, it is important to note that the Marxist analysis is grounded in a broader perspective that takes into account historical materialism and class struggle. Marxists argue that while individuals may find limited success within the confines of capitalism, the system itself perpetuates inequality, exploitation, and class antagonisms that cannot be eradicated without a fundamental transformation of society.

Furthermore, the legacy of Marx and Engels extends beyond their analysis of the working class. Marx's "Communist Manifesto" presented a vision of a classless society where private property and the oppressive exploitation of labor would be abolished. Although their ideas have been misinterpreted and misapplied in various historical contexts, they have also inspired social movements seeking to dismantle oppressive systems and advocate for workers' rights and social justice.

In addition to their critiques of capitalism, Marx and Engels also explored the historical processes and class formations that led to the establishment of capitalism. Marx developed the theory of historical materialism, arguing that economic systems emerge and develop based on the material conditions and productive forces of society. He traced the transition from feudalism to capitalism, highlighting the enclosure of common lands and the emergence of wage labor as crucial elements in the formation of the capitalist mode of production.

Marx also investigated the role of ideology in perpetuating and justifying capitalist exploitation. He argued that dominant ideas within society, including religious, political, and legal systems, are products of the ruling class and serve to maintain their power and control. This concept, known as ideological hegemony, explains how ruling-class ideas become infused in all aspects of society, shaping and influencing collective consciousness.

Moreover, Marx and Engels understood the limitations of social reform within the capitalist system. While they recognized the importance of fighting for immediate improvements in working conditions and workers' rights, they believed that true emancipation could only be achieved through a revolutionary overthrow of capitalism. They advocated for the formation of a conscious and organized working-class movement that would collectively challenge the power structures of capitalism and build a socialist society based on cooperation, equality, and shared ownership of the means of production.

In summary, Marx and Engels provided a deep and incisive critique of capitalism, exposing the underlying contradictions and injustices that define the capitalist mode of production. Their analyses of the working class, alienation, cyclical crises, historical materialism, and ideological hegemony shed light on the multifaceted aspects of capitalist exploitation. By understanding their theories, we can gain valuable insights into the conditions faced by the working class and the urgent need for a more equitable and humane socio-economic system.

Appendix: Timeline of Karl Marx's life, Glossary of Marxist terms, Suggestions for further reading

1818: Karl Marx is born on May 5th in Trier, Germany, to a middle-class family of Jewish descent. His father, Heinrich Marx, was a lawyer and his mother, Henrietta Pressburg, came from a wealthy family. Marx was the third of nine children.

- 1835: Marx enrolls at the University of Bonn to study law, but his interest quickly shifts towards philosophy and literature. He becomes involved in radical student organizations and joins a group of poets known as the Young Hegelians. Marx's studies are disrupted by his rebellious nature, resulting in academic struggles and clashes with authorities.

- 1841: Marx transfers to the University of Berlin to continue his studies in philosophy and sociology. It is during this time that he becomes exposed to the writings of German philosophers such as G.W.F. Hegel and Ludwig Feuerbach, whose ideas greatly influence his own thinking.

- 1843: Marx moves to Paris, driven by the political and intellectual environment of the city. Here, he becomes deeply involved in political journalism and begins writing for radical publications such as the Rheinische Zeitung and Deutsch-Französische Jahrbücher. During this period, Marx also meets Friedrich Engels, who would become his lifelong friend and collaborator.

- 1844: Marx completes his early philosophical manuscripts, known as the Economic and Philosophic Manuscripts of 1844. In these works, he explores concepts such as alienation, labor, and the critique of capitalism. Although these manuscripts are not published during Marx's lifetime, they lay the foundation for his later works.

- 1845: Following the French government's crackdown on radical publications, Marx is forced to leave Paris and moves to Brussels, Belgium. Here, he continues his political activism and starts writing for the German-language socialist newspaper Vorwärts!

- 1848: Marx publishes "The Communist Manifesto" with Friedrich Engels. The manifesto, written in response to the revolutionary tide sweeping across Europe, outlines Marx's theory of historical materialism and advocates for the overthrow of the capitalist system. Despite initial limited reception, it becomes one of the most influential political pamphlets in history.

- 1849: In the wake of the failed revolution in Germany, Marx is expelled from France and settles in London, England, where he would spend the rest of his life. In London, Marx establishes himself as a political thinker and writes for various radical newspapers.

- 1859: Marx publishes his major work "A Contribution to the Critique of Political Economy." In this book, he introduces key concepts such as surplus value and the labor theory of value, providing a critical analysis of capitalist production and the exploitation of labor.

- 1867: Marx publishes the first volume of "Capital: A Critique of Political Economy." This monumental work further develops his critique of capitalism, delving into the capitalist mode of production, commodity fetishism, and the contradictions inherent in capitalist society. Marx's subsequent volumes of "Capital" were published posthumously by Engels based on his notes and manuscripts.

- 1871: Marx closely observes and analyzes the Paris Commune, a short-lived revolutionary government established in Paris, which he sees as a real-life manifestation of the dictatorship of the proletariat. He draws important lessons and insights from this experience, which find their way into his future writings.

- 1881: Marx faces declining health and experiences financial difficulties. However, he continues his intellectual pursuits, corresponding with various socialist leaders and intellectuals around the world.

- 1883: Karl Marx passes away on March 14th in London. Although he did not live to see the full impact of his ideas, his works would go on to shape the course of history, influencing political movements, revolutions, and scholarly debates for generations to come.

Glossary of Marxist Terms:

1. Proletariat: The working class, who do not own the means of production. According to Marx, they are exploited by the bourgeoisie and their labor power generates surplus value.

2. Bourgeoisie: The capitalist class, who own the means of production. They profit by appropriating the surplus value created by the working class.

3. Dialectical Materialism: The philosophical framework in which contradictions and conflicts drive societal changes. Marx's application of dialectics to the material conditions of society formed the basis of his historical materialism.

4. Class Struggle: The conflict between the proletariat and bourgeoisie, believed to be the driving force behind historical change. Marx argued that history is shaped by the struggles between oppressor and oppressed classes.

5. Surplus Value: The difference between the value workers produce and the wages they receive, appropriated by the capitalists. Marx considered this exploitation inherent to capitalist production and central to the accumulation of capital.

6. Historical Materialism: The theory that the structure of society is determined by the development of the productive forces. Marx believed that material conditions and productive relations shape social, political, and cultural institutions.

7. Alienation: The feeling of being disconnected and dehumanized from one's work and the products of one's labor. Under capitalist systems, Marx argues that workers become estranged from their labor and lose control over the fruits of their labor.

8. Socialist Revolution: The overthrow of the capitalist system by the working class to establish a socialist society. Marx believed that the proletariat, with its potential collective power, would lead this revolution against the bourgeoisie.

9. Dictatorship of the Proletariat: A transitional phase between capitalism and communism, in which the working class holds political power. Marx envisioned that the dictatorship of the proletariat would ensure the dismantling of capitalist institutions and the establishment of socialist policies.

10. Communist Society: A classless, stateless society in which private property is abolished and resources are distributed according to need. Marx's ultimate vision was of a communist society where individual freedom and social equality are achieved.

Suggestions for Further Reading:

1. "Capital, Volume I" by Karl Marx.
2. "The Marx-Engels Reader" edited by Robert C. Tucker.
3. "Marx's Capital and Capitalism Today" by Tony Cutler and Barry Hindess. 4. "Marx and Engels' 'German Ideology' Manuscripts" edited by C. J. Arthur.
4. "A Companion to Marx's Capital" edited by David Harvey.
5. "The Marx-Engels-Gesamtausgabe (MEGA): An Annotated Research Guide" by Sven-Eric Liedman.
6. "Marx's Capital and Hegel's Logic: A Reexamination" by Tony Cutler.
7. "Marx's Inferno: The Political Theory of Capital" by William Clare Roberts. 9. "The Marx-Engels Cyclopedia" edited by Charles H. Kerr Publishing Company.
8. "Reading Capital" by Louis Althusser and Étienne Balibar.

9. "Marx's Das Kapital for Beginners" by Michael Wayne.
10. "Karl Marx: Selected Writings" edited by David McLellan.
11. "Marx's Capital and the Earth: An Anti-Critique" by John Bellamy Foster and Paul Burkett.
12. "Marx's Capital and Modernity" by Tony Cutler and Barry Hind.
13. "Marx's Capital and Capitalism Today" by Tony Cutler and Barry Hindess.
14. "Class Struggles in the USSR: First Period (1917-1923)" by Charles Bettelheim.
15. "The Revolutionary Ideas of Karl Marx" by Alex Callinicos.
16. "Marxism in the Age of Globalization" by Mikhail Aleksandrovich Kolyaskin.
17. "Marx, Capital, and the Madness of Economic Reason" by David Harvey
18. "The Marx-Engels Reader" edited by Robert C. Tucker.
19. "A Companion to Marx's Capital" edited by David Harvey.
20. "Karl Marx: Greatness and Illusion" by Gareth Stedman Jones.
21. "Re-Reading Marx: New Perspectives after the Critical Edition" edited by Jan Hoff, He Ping, and Mark E. Blum.
22. "Marx's Capital and Hegel's Logic: A Reexamination" by Tony Cutler.
23. "Marxology: Marx as Political Philosopher" edited by Sergio Luzzatto and Antonello La Vergata.
24. "Marx, Lenin, and the Revolutionary Experience: Studies of Communism and Radicalism in an Age of Globalization" by Paul Le Blanc.
25. "Marx and Engels' 'German Ideology' Manuscripts" edited by C. J. Arthur.
26. "Marx's Inferno: The Political Theory of Capital" by William Clare Roberts.

27. "Marx's Capital and Capitalism Today" by Tony Cutler and Barry Hindess.
28. "Reading Capital" by Louis Althusser and Étienne Balibar.

These books cover a wide range of topics related to Marx's theories, including his critique of capitalism, the role of class struggle, the dynamics of historical change, and the relevance of Marxism in the contemporary world. Whether you are an academic scholar, a student, or simply interested in gaining a deeper understanding of Marx's ideas, these works provide valuable insights and analysis.

Finally, the Marxist Internet Archive is a great source for those who are not yet familiar with Marx and Marxism.

Marxists Internet Archive: https://www.marxists.org

Takeaways

Karl Marx is undoubtedly one of the most influential thinkers in history, whose ideas have shaped the course of social, political, and economic thought. Born on May 5, 1818, in Trier, Germany, Marx's intellectual journey led him to develop a profound critique of capitalist society, unveiling its inherent contradictions and exploitative nature. His vision for a communist society, outlined in works such as The Communist Manifesto and Das Kapital, continues to inspire and provoke debates to this day.

Early Life and Education

Karl Marx was born into a middle-class family, with his father working as a lawyer. Growing up in a comfortable household, his privileged background allowed him access to education and intellectual exploration. From an early age, Marx exhibited a voracious appetite for knowledge and a keen sense of inquiry that would later shape his revolutionary ideas.

Marx's father, Heinrich Marx, was a liberal thinker who encouraged his son's intellectual pursuits. His mother, Henriette Marx, came from a Jewish family, introducing Marx to the rich cultural and historical legacy of Judaism. The intersection of his parents' beliefs and values played a crucial role in shaping Karl Marx's perspective on religion, society, and politics.

In his formative years, Marx enrolled at the Friedrich Wilhelm Gymnasium, where his intellect and academic prowess shone brightly. Excelling in a wide range of subjects, he exhibited a particular affinity for literature, philosophy, and history. Marx's exposure to the Enlightenment thinkers, such as Voltaire and Rousseau, fueled his desire to understand the social and political realities that surrounded him.

Continuing his education at the University of Bonn, Marx initially pursued law, following in the footsteps of his father. However, his true passion resided in the fields of philosophy and literature. During his time at the university, Marx began to immerse himself in political activism, engaging with radical student groups and challenging the conservative societal norms prevailing in academia.

Transferring to the University of Berlin, Marx found himself under the tutelage of the renowned philosopher G.W.F. Hegel. Hegel's dialectical approach and his emphasis on historical analysis had a profound impact on Marx's intellectual development. Immersed in the study of Hegelian philosophy, Marx began to develop his own unique theories that would later form the foundation of his critique of capitalism.

The Formation of Marx's Ideas

Following the completion of his studies, Marx embarked on a career as a journalist and writer, using his platform to disseminate his critiques of the prevailing political and economic system. Engaging with various intellectual currents of his era, including the Young Hegelians and the socialist movement, he integrated their ideas into his evolving theoretical framework.

Marx's engagement with the Young Hegelians, a group of radical intellectuals influenced by Hegel, allowed him to refine his theory of historical materialism. Departing from Hegel's idealism, Marx emphasized the pivotal role of material conditions and economic relations as the driving forces behind social change. This departure marked a crucial turning point in his intellectual journey.

Furthermore, Marx delved into the study of classical political economy, meticulously examining the works of Adam Smith and David Ricardo. Through his critical evaluation, he identified the theoretical gaps within their theories of value, exchange, and profit.

In response, Marx formulated his labor theory of value, arguing that the value of a commodity is determined by the socially necessary labor time required to produce it. This labor theory of value underscored the exploitative nature of capitalist relations of production.

Marx's Critique of Capitalism

At the core of Marx's critique of capitalism lies his analysis of its inherent contradictions and exploitative nature. Through his writings, Marx delves into various aspects of the capitalist system, exposing its structural flaws and highlighting the injustices that pervade it.

One of Marx's key insights is the notion of alienation, whereby workers are estranged from the products of their labor and from their own creative potential. Under capitalism, workers are reduced to mere commodities, selling their labor power in exchange for a wage. This alienated relationship to labor dehumanizes individuals and strips them of their autonomy and fulfillment.

Marx also critiques the process of commodification, which transforms everything, including labor, into a commodity for exchange in the market. This commodification reduces labor to a mere object that can be bought and sold, distorting social relations and leading to the fetishization of commodities.

Moreover, Marx scrutinizes the capitalist accumulation process, highlighting the exploitation of labor embedded within it. He argues that capitalists extract surplus value from workers by paying them less than the value of the goods and services they produce. This surplus value is then appropriated by the capitalist class, perpetuating inequality and reinforcing class divisions.

Marx's analysis of capitalism not only reveals its flaws but also highlights the potential for revolutionary transformation. He posits that capitalism itself contains the seeds of its own destruction, as the working class, or proletariat, becomes increasingly marginalized and alienated. Marx believes that through their collective struggle, the proletariat will rise against the bourgeoisie, leading to the establishment of a classless society.

The Communist Manifesto

In 1848, Marx and his collaborator Friedrich Engels published The Communist Manifesto, a seminal work that outlines their theory of historical class struggles and calls for the overthrow of the capitalist system. The Manifesto serves as a rallying cry for the working class, urging them to recognize their collective power and to unite for revolution.

The Manifesto traces the historical development of society as a series of class struggles. Marx and Engels argue that throughout history, societies have been characterized by the dominance of one class over another, leading to various forms of oppression and exploitation. In the capitalist era, the bourgeoisie emerged as the ruling class, exploiting the proletariat and perpetuating social inequality.

According to Marx and Engels, the bourgeoisie's insatiable drive for profit and accumulation leads to the constant revolutionizing of society and the destabilization of traditional social relations. However, they contend that capitalism ultimately engenders its own downfall, as the proletariat becomes increasingly conscious of their exploitation and the necessity for revolutionary change.

The Manifesto delineates ten immediate demands to be pursued by the working class, including the abolition of property in land, a progressive tax system, and free public education. Marx and Engels also emphasize the international nature of the labor movement, calling for the international solidarity of the working class.

The impact of The Communist Manifesto cannot be understated. It has served as a catalyst for countless revolutionary movements throughout history, from the Russian Revolution to the struggles for independence in colonized nations. Its ideas continue to resonate with those seeking social justice and an alternative to the exploitative nature of capitalism.

References:

1. Marx, Karl, and Friedrich Engels. The Communist Manifesto. Penguin Classics, 2002.
2. Bottomore, Tom. Karl Marx: Selected Writings in Sociology and Social Philosophy. McGraw-Hill Education, 2012.
3. McLellan, David. Karl Marx: A Biography. Palgrave Macmillan, 2006.
4. Harvey, David. A Companion to Marx's Capital. Verso, 2010.
5. Sperber, Jonathan. Karl Marx: A Nineteenth-Century Life. W.W. Norton & Company, 2013.
6. Tucker, Robert C. The Marx-Engels Reader.Chapter 2: The Legacy of Marx's Ideas

Marx's ideas have had a lasting impact on a wide range of disciplines, including sociology, economics, political science, and philosophy. His critique of capitalism, analysis of social class, and vision of a communist society continue to shape academic discourse and influence political movements around the world.

Marxist Sociology

Marx's emphasis on the social relations of production and the class struggle laid the foundation for Marxist sociology. This branch of sociology examines how social structures and economic systems shape social behavior and the distribution of power. Marxist sociologists analyze society through the lens of class conflict, focusing on the socioeconomic inequalities that arise from the capitalist mode of production.

One key concept in Marxist sociology is class consciousness, which refers to the awareness of one's position in the class structure and the understanding of common interests and shared experiences with others in the same class. Class consciousness plays a crucial role in mobilizing the working class to challenge capitalist exploitation and advocate for social change.

Marxist Economics

Marx's economic theories have had a profound impact on the field of economics, particularly in the critique of capitalism and the analysis of the capitalist mode of production. His labor theory of value, as mentioned earlier, argues that the value of a commodity depends on the socially necessary labor time required to produce it.

Marxist economists also focus on the concept of surplus value, which refers to the excess value created by workers beyond what they are paid in wages. Marx argues that capitalists profit from this surplus value and accumulate wealth at the expense of the working class. This analysis of exploitation has led to debates and discussions on economic inequality and the distribution of wealth in society.

Political Science and Marxism

Marx's ideas have also influenced political science, particularly in discussions on power, ideology, and social change. Marxist political theory highlights the role of economic forces and class struggle in shaping political institutions and ideologies. It emphasizes the ways in which state power is used to protect and advance the interests of the ruling class.

Marxists argue that the state can never truly represent the interests of the proletariat, as it is inevitably dominated by the bourgeoisie. They advocate for the overthrow of the capitalist state and its replacement with a socialist or communist system, where power is held and exercised collectively by the working class.

Marxist Philosophy

Marx's philosophy, heavily influenced by Hegelian dialectics, offers a unique framework for understanding historical and social change. His dialectical materialism posits that change occurs through the conflict of opposing forces, driven by contradictions within society. This perspective has shaped critical theory, which seeks to uncover the underlying power dynamics and ideological structures that perpetuate social inequality and oppression.

One of the central tenets of Marxist philosophy is praxis, the alignment of theory and practice. Marx believed that theory should inform action and that understanding the material conditions of society should lead to efforts to transform it. This emphasis on praxis has motivated countless social movements and revolutionaries who seek to enact societal change based on Marxist principles.

Critiques and Debates

While Marx's ideas have undoubtedly had a profound impact, there are also a number of critiques and debates surrounding his theories. Some criticisms argue that Marx's analysis of class struggle and historical materialism overlooks other important social factors such as race, gender, and culture. Critics also contend that his predictions about the inevitable collapse of capitalism have not come to fruition.

Additionally, there have been debates about the role of the state in Marxist theory. Some argue that the state can be a tool for progressive change, while others believe that it is inherently tied to capitalist interests and cannot be used to facilitate a transition to socialism or communism.

Despite these criticisms and debates, Marx's ideas continue to resonate and inspire, particularly in times of economic crises, social unrest, and political upheaval. The quest for a more equitable and just society remains at the heart of Marxist thought, sparking ongoing discussions and movements for social change.

Conclusion

Karl Marx's brilliance as a thinker and his profound impact on history cannot be overstated. His critiques of capitalism, analysis of social class, and vision for a communist society continue to shape academic fields and influence political movements. Marx's ideas have prompted reflection on the inherent contradictions and exploitative nature of capitalism, as well as the potential for revolutionary transformation. While his work is not free from criticism, it remains a vital and enduring body of thought that continues to inspire and provoke debate.

About the Author

Hichem Karoui is a social scientist, researcher, political analyst, consultant, novelist, poet, English-Arabic Editor-in-Chief and author or co-author of fifty published books and numerous academic or media articles. He holds a PhD in Sociology from The Sorbonne University (Paris III).

Experience:

- Founder and Director of GEW Reports & Analyses (The Voice of the Mediterranean), a France-based think tank and Online publishing platform.

- Researcher and Consultant for "Underscore Media" in Abu Dhabi (2019-February 2023).

- Director of the Gulf Future Center in London (January 2020 - October 2022).

- Non-resident Senior Fellow and academic adviser at various institutions in China (2019-2021).

- Researcher and Consultant at the Diplomatic Institute, Doha (2013-2019).

- Associate Researcher at the Arab Center for Research and Policy Studies, Doha (2011-2013).

- Researcher at the Sorbonne University's Centre for Contemporary Oriental Studies, Paris (2009-2011).

- Journalist, commentator, Editor-in-Chief, political analyst, and columnist (1981-2019).

Scholarly Publications:

- Author of multiple books on various topics, including On China And the Arabs, The Political Algebra of Global Value Change, Power Revolving Doors , Self-Improvement, What is Happiness, Middle East Studies in the USA, Inventing The Middle East, etc.

- Published numerous articles and research papers in peer-reviewed journals and international conferences.

He has also written several literary works, such as the serialised novel "The Morning of the Mogul."

In addition to his academic and literary pursuits, Karoui has worked as a journalist, commentator, editor-in-chief, political analyst, and daily or weekly columnist in Arabic and English for various media outlets in the Arab world, Europe, the United States, and China.

Academic Degrees:

- PhD in Sociology, Sorbonne University (Paris 3).

- MA in Middle Eastern and Mediterranean Studies, Sorbonne University (Paris 3).

- Maitrise (Master 1) in English Language, Literature, and Civilisation, Sorbonne University (Paris 3).

- Maitrise (Master 1) in Arabic Language, Literature, and Civilisation, Sorbonne University (Paris 3).

Read more at https://hichemkaroui.net.

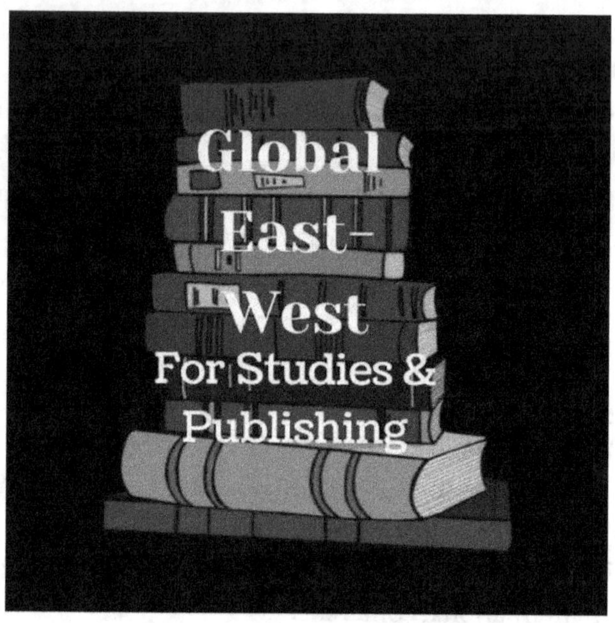

About the Publisher

We are a group of passionate individuals who believe in the power of education and knowledge sharing. We have come together to form this company to make a difference in the lives of others.

Our mission is to promote understanding and cooperation between people of different cultures and backgrounds. We publish books and other resources that provide accurate and unbiased information about different cultures and countries.

We believe education is the key to a better future for all of us.

Global East West For Studies & Publishing is an imprint of Global East-West LTD, a company registered in London (UK) under the number **13930095**.

We publish Ebooks and Books, Fiction and Non-Fiction, monographs, essays, etc.

For any request, please email: info@global-east-west.co.uk
https://global-east-west.co.uk/